GAME ON
ALL THE TIME

GROWING UP IN THE HOME OF A
LEGENDARY FOOTBALL COACH:

L. R. NELSON

To John,
I hope
you enjoy
my
book.

by Dan Nelson, Pastor
First Baptist Church of
Camarillo, California

Dan
Nelson

Daniel
12:3

FAITHFUL LIFE
PUBLISHERS & PRINTERS

Game On All the Time
Growing Up in the Home of a Legendary Football Coach: L. R. Nelson

Copyright © 2017 by Dan Nelson

Paperback ISBN: 978-1-63073-171-7

eBook ISBN: 978-1-63073-187-8

Faithful Life Publishers & Printers
North Fort Myers, FL 33903

FaithfulLifePublishers.com
info@FaithfulLifePublishers.com
888.720.0950

20 19 18 17   1 2 3 4 5

BACK COVER PICTURE

Captured in time is the best moment of Agricola High School Football up to that point. Finishing their 3rd season and the 2nd under Daddy as coach, they are awarded the Camellia Bowl Trophy in Lucedale, Mississippi for beating the Richton Rebels 32-12, finishing with a 9-2 record despite the memorable loss to Rocky Creek.

Acknowledgments

I would like to thank my brothers David, Donald and Darwin for their assistance in recalling stories they had of our Dad, the teams he coached and students he taught. They helped me with the accuracy of the stories, scores and records. Growing up we worked together as a team and their teamwork helped me tremendously collecting stories about our Dad.

Thanks to Virginia Watson, a dear member of First Baptist Church of Camarillo and former church secretary who assisted me in reading the manuscript and offered suggestions.

I would like to thank Amy Cranage, Administrative Assistant at First Baptist Church of Camarillo who helped immensely in editing the book, especially in punctuation, sentence structure and proper use of words.

A special thank you is extended to my wife Janice, not only with her help in editing but also with the use of names referenced in this book.

Thank you to my church at First Baptist Camarillo, CA, who has encouraged me and has been supportive of my writing ministry.

And of course last but not least, thank-you to former students, players and people who knew my Father and Mother and provided encouragement to write this book. Positive responses to these stories on Facebook in their rough version, were encouraging. Several have told me, "You must publish this book." Others kept asking when it was going to be published. I'm glad our wait is over.

Disclaimer Statement

All stories in the *Game On All the Time* are accurate as to their authenticity. I cannot vouch for every detail being completely correct since they were collected from several sources.

Any reference to actual people whether they are mentioned by name or referred to anonymously was not intended to be derogatory in any sense. They are part of the actual narrative of the story and cherished memories.

Endorsements and Memories of my Father: L. R. Nelson

As a player on the 1968 East Central High School Football Team, I have some fond memories of Coach Nelson. He not only coached our team, but also managed his players. He knew each player's strengths and weaknesses. His plays were designed to amplify our strengths and at practice we worked on our weaknesses. He used to say, "You can't get better if you don't practice."

— Bruce Holmberg, football player at East Central High School 1968

I loved him. I was the office aid for he and Coach Shirley in the guidance office in 1979/80; never a dull moment with those two. They definitely fit into the legends columns at East Central!

— Laura Porter Whittington, former student Aid East Central High School

My husband Lonnie and I graduated in 1969 and were both in Coach Nelson's home room and class. We have fond memories of him. Obviously, he was loved by more than just the East Central Football Team. He had a ready smile, but he could also be stern when needed. A small girl myself, I never wanted to do anything to cause me to be the recipient of Coach Nelson's legendary paddle. I was not alone; the biggest boys were in awe of that paddle and the coach behind it! What wonderful days when teachers, coaches and band directors were free to guide, instruct, discipline, lift and care for students in ways that still make a difference 50 years later!

> — **Mary S. Slider, former student East Central High School 1969**

Thank you for bringing back memories which many have long forgotten. They were wonderfully revived in your sharing these stories of the school and community in which I grew up.

> — **Linda Holland, former student at Agricola High School**

I got the opportunity to play ball for Coach in '71, the best year I ever had! Your Dad and Coach Shirley motivated me and always brought out the best in me on the field.

> — **Tommy Eldridge, football player at East Central High School. 1971.**

There was a lot of hard work involved in playing for L.R. He taught us many things about football and winning, but most of all he taught us how to be successful in life. If you look across the community, the athletes that he touched have had a very positive life. We had many fun times also. I was usually the brunt of his pranks which included wearing a baby diaper that he pinned on me at practice and wearing a baby pacifier around my neck all practice. We always got off early on Wednesday for prayer meeting and the Red Skelton show.

> — **Mike Long, football player at East Central 1966-1968.**

We had been practicing on the girls' basketball team and I had not been able to make a goal to save my life. With him being coach, he was not happy with me. Then out of the blue I finally did just what he had been after me to do. Feeling a little better about myself, here he came and I was thinking by the look on his face that I must not have done something right. He approached me and exclaimed, "That's what I want!" You could have knocked me over. There was a sense of accomplishment that I had been able to do what I was not able to do before.

He was a great coach. He loved all sports as far as I knew, and he wanted his players to give their all. He gave his all as their coach. I had a great deal of respect for him as a student and later as years passed that respect was always there.

— Lynn Baker Thompson, former student and player at Agricola High School in the 1960's

I would first like to say That I consider it an honor and a privilege to have the opportunity to express my feelings and share some memories about a man who meant so much to me as a young high school football player and student at Agricola High School. L.R. Nelson came to Agricola High School as a history teacher and head football coach when I was in the ninth grade.

Coach Nelson taught me American History and I remember him being a very strict disciplinarian. He made American History interesting and very real to his students by teaching us about the greatness of the United States of America. He was a veteran who had served our country during World War II in the U.S. Navy.

Coach Nelson was my football coach all four years at Agricola High School. He told us that he believed that the game of football was like life—sometimes you fall down or get knocked down, but you have to pick yourself up and start all over.

During football practice, Coach Nelson was a very close observer of everything that took place on the field. He would not hesitate to correct our mistakes as he saw fit. His philosophy was: Know the plays, be physically fit, play smart and follow the rules of the game. He taught us that football is a team sport and that every player had a part. Eleven players executing together, knowing their plays, physically in shape, playing smart and following the rules of the game will win football games and it did!

As I think back on those high school years, I realize how blessed we as students and football players were to have someone like Coach Nelson in our lives, who meant so much and really cared for each of us.

A friend for life and a world of memories to never be forgotten.

> — **Jimmy Vise, former student and player at Agricola High School 1958-1962**

What a wonderful man he was! I was there for the Pickle Bowl year! As well has 1971! Coach Nelson was a wise man! I loved him as a teacher and a friend. He used to go fishing with my brothers, what a time they had!

> — **Beverly Ellerbe Leonard, former East Central High School student**

My senior year, I was an office aid for him when he was a guidance counselor. Not only was he a great coach, he also was an encourager! I witnessed him counseling students about their grades (even tutoring some of them who struggled). He also worked diligently to help those who wanted to go to college find a way to get there. He was a fine man who I was honored to know!

> — **Penny Stork Dearman, former East Central High School student and Office Aid**

Coach L.R. Nelson was a motivational leader and master mentor for young men. Coach Nelson was all of these things to the young men who attended Agricola High School. He was our Coach, Boy Scoutmaster and our Sunday School Teacher. No pun intended: We couldn't get away from him!

He taught us about life in more ways than I can remember. He would say, "Competition will make you successful in the game of life." He instilled in us what it took to be successful, no matter what we attempted.

One of the things he cared about the most, was building character in us. One of his favorite sayings was, "I'm not interested in what happens Friday night. I am interested in what kind of person you are when you're 25 years old." I think many of the young men he associated with still heed that advice.

> — **Ronnie Pierce, Starting Quarterback of the undefeated Agricola High School Football Team in 1963 and My Father's Successor as Head Coach of the East Central High School Football Team 1971**

TABLE OF CONTENTS

Foreword

On a Friday night in October you can drive through almost any small southern town and wonder where the people are. It is almost as though the people have been taken away and only a few signs of life are detectable. Then suddenly in the distance, you see lights at the far end of town. As you drive closer, you realize these are lights to the local high school football field. That is when you realize where everyone in the town has gone. They have all fled to see the local team do battle with a rival or another familiar team. Such is the life of a small town when it comes to high school football. The Friday night football game is the place to be. It is the staple of the community and all anyone can talk about. From the school where the players wear their jerseys all day at school (as if they weren't noticeable enough already), to the local stores and businesses where everyone lives and dies with the success of the local high school football team.

I was privileged to be right in the center of that activity, along with my brothers as we grew up in the home of the local head football coach: L.R. Nelson. He wasn't just any Dad. Instead, he was the most recognizable figure in the community besides the pastor. You just called him "Coach" and everyone knew who you were referring to. The fall was his season to shine as the coach of most of the young men who went to school in Agricola, a little farming community that came alive during football season.

Daddy wasn't just any football coach either. He was a motivator and leader who seemed to get the most of his teams although they weren't expected to do that well on some particular year. My brothers and I were greatly influenced by him and he left a positive impression on many in that community. Daddy loved hunting, fishing, and most of all football. In the fall when everyone's thoughts turned to the season, he was right in the middle of the football team. He lived it, breathed it and went through the season in a manner reminiscent of a general preparing and executing a battle plan in a war.

We lived in the glory days of the short-lived Agricola High School football program. They were wonderful days. It was like the season was just stuck in time and was there for us to enjoy and be excited about. We never forgot about football. We counted the days till the next game, recorded the score, knew the starting lineups, looked forward to the next opponent, somehow managed to attend school and somewhat study. We went through the schedule with Daddy in a manner one can hardly guess any coach's family could have.

When we weren't going to the games or traveling to the away games (which weren't too far away), we played ball ourselves. From playing at recess when we were little to eventually becoming players on the teams Daddy coached, our days were fun and filled with excitement. Daddy used the same motivation to excite his team, in the home we were raised. He believed in our potential, whether it was in sports, hunting, fishing, working or just life, period.

The Baptist Church anchored us to God's Word in our spiritual life, but Daddy was the anchor of our home. He was that example of how a father instructs, disciplines and leads the family.

Being around my Dad, one couldn't help but catch his enthusiasm for what was his primary interest at that time. We were proud to be in the home of Coach Nelson as his sons and it yielded memories we will never forget.

When you peer into the home of a man like this there is one expression that comes to my mind to describe our home life: *Game On all the Time*. Our boyhood years were a series of activities centering around school, church, and sports. We were never bored because the game was always on. Daddy kept us motivated to live life as if we were giving it our all for four quarters. The enthusiasm for sports in rural South Mississippi was exemplified through our Dad. He kept us going, growing, and motivated in everything we did.

It is altogether fitting and proper to hang this title on the book before you, which I have put together with the help of my brothers' recollections. For the game never ended in our lives, regardless of where we went with our careers and residences. We were always competing and never stopped competing. Daddy taught us not to quit, or at least never admit failure. Those lessons may have been imprinted in our DNA by genetics, but these were also ingrained in us because he instructed through the example of his life. He was the one who sparked enthusiasm in others and especially in us.

I thought it would be helpful to provide insight into what motivates those who are in a home with a father like ours. If given a glimpse of these factors, you will realize why football is integral, especially in small towns down South. This motivation is why everyone is at the football game, anticipates the season, and is saddened after the final game. But we did not have to worry about the end of the season blues in our house, for the game was on all the time. This is the story about that game and the influence of our Dad who was the man who never stopped coaching even when he went home.

WHY THIS BOOK?

We gathered around that little home where I grew up awaiting the eventual passing of our Dad. I had rushed in from California where I have served as pastor of a church for over three decades. My brother Donald had picked me up from the airport in New Orleans and we drove back to Agricola, Mississippi, which is in George County. It's a small farming community in South Mississippi just north of the Mississippi Gulf Coast, located between Hattiesburg, Mississippi, and Mobile, Alabama.

On the drive, there, Donald called several times to see how Daddy was doing, only to learn that his condition was worsening as he slipped into a comatose state. They were switching him to a hospital bed when we finally walked inside. Cars surrounded the little house where I had grown up as a child. We entered the house to see dozens of people standing in the living room with hardly enough breathing room for everyone. The hospice nurse was explaining the dying process to my other two brothers. We knew Daddy would pass away sometime within the next few days, although it seemed unfathomable.

Despite all this inevitability surrounding us, it was not an ominous occasion for many friends and former students gathered there to say good-bye. What followed in the next few days was incredible. People whose lives were influenced by Daddy, those he had taught or coached, came by and offered their memorable stories about him as well as my mother. She had been a teacher and a figure in the community in her own right. My mother had been bedridden because of the massive strokes that left her completely incapacitated during Daddy's final days.

We did what only seemed natural. We began telling stories about Daddy and there were so many! I caught myself after I had shared a couple of stories, reminding myself of the somberness of the occasion. Nevertheless, the present pastor of Agricola Baptist Church said, "Keep going! I'm really enjoying this." That was when I realized there were so many stories about Daddy in every place he had coached and taught. There were stories everywhere he had interacted with students, players, and teachers. Why were there so many stories? It was because he had influenced so many people in his "down to earth" and unpretentious manner. He loved being around people and people loved being around him.

Daddy was an avid sportsman as a hunter and angler. He had coached everything from football to track and everything in between. He was also a motivator of people and while he may not have been Knute Rockne, he knew how to get the best out of his players. A look at the football teams he coached provided an understanding of his drive to push them to the height of their potential. He got the most out of every team that played for him, more so than many coaches would have been able to accomplish. He made his players think of themselves as winners in whatever sport he coached. Almost anyone could say, "I played for Coach Nelson, and he helped me believe I could do anything."

Instead of trying to remember all these stories years later, I decided to put pen to paper to recall the places he coached and the stories associated with him as a coach and friend. I called my brothers for their help in this quest to find all these stories which spanned different eras of our lives concerning the teams and players they recalled that he coached. My three younger brothers all live in close proximity to one another in Southern Mississippi, at the place our father held forth for so long in his job as coach, teacher, scoutmaster, Sunday school teacher, and where he led a great example of what it means to be a Dad. The purpose in writing this book is to hopefully give you some insight into the positive role model my Dad was as a parent, for we all need father's like Coach Nelson.

* * * * * * * * * *

Throughout the book, you will find three groups of pictures which help to highlight Daddy's incredible life.

Pages 29-31, 63-66 and 107-109

Detailed captions for these pictures are located on pages 138-140.

1.

BACKGROUND: How My Father Grew up and Became a Coach

Lorie Robinson Nelson was born April 5, 1926 in Haynesville, Louisiana. His family on his mother's side had called the Louisiana town on the Arkansas border, their home for several generations. His Grandfather had been an influential person in the community and his father, Charles, was a wildcat oil rigger from East Texas who met Verna Lou, his wife, on a job while in Haynesville. Lorie was the oldest of three children and had a younger brother and sister; Carol and Carolyn, who were fraternal twins. Lorie never really liked his name and he reminded us of it a lot when we were growing up. His mother must have wanted a girl, but the name did not suit my Dad. From the early days, he went by Lorie but later switched to L.R. during his high school and naval career. He went by Coach Nelson throughout his coaching career and into his retirement. He also had several nicknames throughout his life. In his coaching days, because of his hard practices and relentless coaching style, he was called "Thug." In his retirement, he was known as "The Old Pro." He even had a bumper sticker on his car indicating this latter nickname, which he must have liked through its display. "The Old Pro" was the familiar character in the old-time beer commercials that we were familiar with, although we never had any liquor in our house and lived in a dry county.

L.R. was born in Haynesville, and lived in several Northern Louisiana towns that were along the present I-20 corridor west and east of Monroe in what is present day Duck Dynasty territory.

Although his parents came back to Haynesville for retirement, he never lived there again.

L.R.'s parents primarily settled in Jackson, Mississippi, but his Dad (my granddaddy) moved from one United Gas Pumping Station to another in my Dad's childhood and early youth. Charlie (L.R.'s Dad), developed a hearing problem after being around the noisy equipment of the pumping station all his life. Lorie went to Central High School in Jackson, Mississippi, and was more of a quite person who was not very popular. He never played on any sports team, even though he was a great sportsman. His father took him and his brother, Carol, hunting and fishing from his early childhood, creating in them a love for these early pastimes all his life. It is odd that my Daddy never had plans to be a coach and it is not inaccurate to say that coaching was one of the furthest things from his mind during his high school days.

Actually, Sports were secondary in 1944 when Daddy graduated from high school. The main concern preoccupying his thinking, as well as every young man of that time, was World War II. Recruitment to serve their country and win the war abroad was why the majority of young men in my Dad's day joined the military in masses. L.R. enlisted in the Navy and was on a destroyer: The U.S.S. McCalla in the Pacific. He was trained as a member of a gunnery team on the torrent guns. He wore long gloves up to his shoulders taking the shell casings out of the gun fired and saw several episodes of combat targeting Kamikaze airplanes which the Japanese used to try and crash into the fleet of ships moving toward Japan in the waning days of the war.

Daddy got into the war during its latter stages and it wasn't long until it came to a sudden halt with the dropping of the bomb and Japan's surrender marking the end of the conflict. When he had returned to his home L.R.'s parents had moved to a rural area in Perry County, Mississippi, to a place called Runnelstown.

With a lot of time on their hands, L.R. and his brother, Carol, learned to play the guitar on their front porch—Merle Travis and Chet Atkins style. They also had time to date certain local girls and L.R. became very interested in Irma Lois Odom, a local girl who was a single schoolteacher there at Runnelstown Elementary School. She was a graduate from Jones Jr. College in Ellisville, Mississippi, and later Mississippi Southern in nearby Hattiesburg. Her father had a farm there on the edge of town and Lorie began to date her while attending school at Mississippi Southern University. Many teachers in South Mississippi graduated from "Southern" which yielded a large teaching corps throughout the state after the war. Although not involved in sports then, Daddy must have thrilled to the coaching skills of legendary Thad "Pie" Van at Mississippi Southern and his star running back Bubba Phillips who later played Major League Baseball.

My parents were married in 1947 at Hattiesburg and attended school as a married couple. Daddy graduated from Mississippi Southern University shortly before I was born in 1951. Hattiesburg was the hub for us, since my parents lived close by with their first teaching positions at Union Elementary School and later at Moselle High and Elementary School for their first permanent jobs together as a married couple. L.R.'s parents moved back to Jackson, but his entire teaching and coaching career was in South Mississippi.

Coaching came by accident to my Dad, who never intended to be a coach. He was a social studies teacher and was very influential in my life-long interest in all kinds of history; particularly Church History and the Civil War.

The principal of the small Moselle High School; Thomas T. Murphree (nicknamed Tree Top), saw in my Dad the possibility of a coach for their little football team. They only had just enough players to field a team and most went both ways on offense and defense. What began though, accidentally, was the beginning of a 20-year coaching career for my Dad. He never talked much about his record or anything at Moselle and I was too young to remember anything. His time there really wasn't anything noteworthy, besides it being the inauguration of his coaching career and I guess that's really important since he had no ambition to be a coach before then. Although I don't know much about his coaching experience at Moselle, he must have liked it in that little school where they needed a football coach.

2.

EARLY ASSISTANT COACHING DAYS

T.T. Murphree (the principal that had pushed Daddy into a not so aspiring coaching career) moved to Leakesville, Mississippi, in Greene County. There he invited my Dad to come to the school after two years at Moselle as a high school football coach and history teacher. My mother taught sixth grade at the elementary school and David was the brother born after me in 1955. Like it or not, Daddy now had a long coaching career ahead of him that he really did not complain much about. In fact, he was getting all into this coaching thing judging by his heightened interest in the sport.

The move to Leakesville was interesting to say the least. We lived in two rental houses for the five years we were there in that small little town, that despite its size was the county seat of Greene County. Greene County which was noted for its deer hunting, was much to Daddy's liking as he would go hunting every fall at a friend's house that was by an area heavily populated by deer. He killed three deer one season, in one afternoon which was the memorable event in his deer hunting time there.

Greene County, with Leakesville as the county seat was an out of the way place bordering the Alabama state line. Its claim to sports fame was a baseball pitcher who hailed from Vinegar Bend, a little place right on the state line. He made it to the majors and pitched for the St. Louis Cardinals, which was the closest major league baseball team to the south back then and he wore the nickname "Vinegar Bend" Mizelle.

Hugh McGinnis, a football player that Daddy coached in Leakesville played for several pro teams. Leakesville High School had a good basketball program for girls, but the football teams usually had either losing seasons or barely won half their games. Daddy coached with three head coaches: Ned Dillard, Cliff Coggin, and Brooks Tisdale. Coggin was a famous player for Mississippi Southern in his college career. Tisdale was successful in other schools after coaching at Leakesville. We maintained our closest friendship through the years with the Dillard's, who had children our age and with whom we were to stay in touch for most of our lives. Each coach tried his best and went on to have successful coaching careers in other places, but not at Leakesville. The lack of deep talent and a small sports program in a small town did not do much to further their coaching careers.

I remember going to the field house when I was a preschooler. The distinct smell and the good-natured kidding is something I will always remember. Sometimes I would stand on the old blocking sleds and the blockers would give me a ride. My Dad had me throwing a football and I remember him holding my hands, while standing behind me showing me how to hit and pitch a baseball. The coaches and players joked with me and even offered me a chaw of tobacco, but Daddy got to me before I could put any in my mouth.

I do recall from an early age the drama of high school football in Mississippi. It was the most exciting thing in town that week, when the school and town came alive on Friday nights. I especially remember the homecoming events and the parades through the middle of town homecoming week with the marching bands leading the way. The schools were so small that players acted as escorts for the homecoming court in their football uniforms at half time. It always looked strange to me for a dirty old football player to be escorting a young girl dressed up like royalty.

Daddy did really well as a girls' basketball coach, and had some good teams with whom he helped reach their potential, featuring some talented girls. They only played half court with the offense and defense on separate halves of the court back then. The area witnessed a modern-day Hoosiers story in girls' basketball when a small little school in George County at Agricola won the 1956 Girl's State Basketball Championship. It was a landmark and stuck with the school as a great accomplishment even after Daddy became the head football coach there.

Bears' football was a different story. Leakesville was not a career-altering place where coaches stayed a long time. When we left in the summer of 1958, the composite total of the games played when Daddy was there featured losing more games than the team won. Although they had a few good seasons, the teams just did not seem to have enough talent to win the Desoto Conference. There were only a few good athletes and winning was always a premium in football at Mississippi high schools.

The '56 season was about the best season the team had, losing only 2 or 3 games as I remember. However, the '57 season was a disaster; so disgusting was the play of the team they did not win a single game. Everyone was disappointed at the team's failure to win at least one game. The coaches actually made the team work out until the Thanksgiving holiday to earn their letter jackets. Everyone knew at the end of the season changes would be made for the next year and changes were made, particularly at the coaching level.

Although Daddy had success with winning teams in girls' basketball, it was not enough to hold a job with the football misery. At the end of the school year, all the coaches were dismissed, creating a particularly hard time for our family. Teacher's pay in Mississippi was the lowest in the nation and my parents certainly did not teach for 40 years there for the money.

My Dad had supplemented his salary working for the State Highway Department in the summer. During the school year; my grandparents lived with us for a while and took care of my brother David and me. We had another brother on the way with no place to live. Daddy had coaching blood in him though and wanted to coach somewhere. Things were about to change however, as we moved south to a memorable place where we were primarily raised.

TOP LEFT: Daddy's World War II Naval painting

TOP RIGHT: Newly wed picture

LEFT: A Great day of deer hunting

BELOW: Leakesville Girl's Basketball Team

ABOVE: Daddy, Mama, Aunt Willie and Uncle Carol

LEFT: First family picture in Agricola

BOTTOM: First Agricola Football Team '58

ABOVE: Pee Wee Team lined up outside
BELOW: Pee Wee Team in the gym

ABOVE: Foots Davis running through a big hole

3.

THE FOOTBALL GLORY DAYS AT AGRICOLA AND EAST CENTRAL

The summer of 1958, we moved to George County, Mississippi and into a small little farming community called Agricola. The word for Agricola in Latin means "farmer."[1] Agricola was eventually the place my parents lived permanently and we always considered it our home. My brother Donald was born in 1958, and we grew up in this small, but very wholesome place to raise a family. Agricola featured a Baptist church that was the center of the community and both my parents received baptism there after professing their faith in Christ. Our new home was where I became a Christian and where I was baptized, called to preach, licensed and ordained in the Agricola Baptist Church. My Dad was there for me during my formative years as Sunday school teacher and scoutmaster. He later taught me in school, after my mother had been my teacher a few years earlier when I was in the fourth grade.

My brothers got involved in sports and I progressed through Little League, Babe Ruth League, High School, and eventually to College Baseball. Both my parents taught at the Agricola School, which consolidated with other small county high schools in the fall of 1964. The five years of coaching at Agricola High School were the solidifying years of my Daddy's football coaching career before the school's consolidation into the county seat school in Lucedale.

---

1 (Meaning of the Word Agricola): https://en.wiktionary.org/wiki/agricola which references: Lewis, Charlton, T. An Elementary Latin Dictionary. New York, Cincinnati, and Chicago, American Book Company, 1890.

The school only had one year, to speak of, in high school football when my Dad became coach. They had only won one game the year before against another team, who had only one win themselves and like Agricola, had lost all their other games. Agricola had only a few players and was really more of a basketball school by virtue of it being the only sport for so many years and the girls' team reputation of winning the State Championship in girls' basketball only three years earlier.

Daddy used to joke about his first year as football coach in Agricola. He told how he initially opened up the ball bin and nothing but basketballs fell out. There was only one football in the bin from where the basketballs fell out, and it was flat. Uniforms were old and ragged and some of the headgear were antiquated, featuring the old leather helmets they used to wear in the beginning stages of football when it was catching on as a sport. There seemed to be a long way to go in the football program and it did not appear they would get there any time soon.

The goal, the first year was to have a winning season and miraculously Daddy had a 6-win 4-loss season. The team matured as they went through the year and great things seemed to be in store for the following year.

The '59 season brought a promising team with only one loss heading toward the end of the season. Our archrivals Rocky Creek (another school on the Northeast corner of the county), was the team Agricola had to beat if they were to win the Singing River Conference. My Dad (knowing how much they wanted to win), told my mother and me that if we didn't beat Rocky Creek we'd have to leave town, he would be fired, and his coaching career would be all over. I believed him so that when the Bulldogs beat us on the last play of the game I thought Daddy would be fired and we were gone. I didn't know if Daddy would be fired immediately or at the end of the year but I sure hated to leave.

As it turned out, my Dad was just teasing and he was retained as the coach after they won the Camellia Bowl in nearby Lucedale. The contest was Agricola's first bowl game ever in this inaugural event. Daddy's team beat Richton 32-12 and finished with a 9 and 2 record, leaving a season that was a remarkable one considering it was only the school's third football season.

The seasons in '60 thru '62 featured winning records for Daddy's teams, which did much for the morale of the school and proved that the '59 season was no fluke. The school only had 20 to 25 students at most in each class from 1st through 12th grade. Technically, half the boys played on the High School football team and there was an even higher percentage in 7th and 8th grade teams. There was only about 500 to 600 people in the community proper, making it a small place where everyone knew everybody and everything about everybody. Agricola, though, had a winning football program despite these limitations. The teams in '60 through '62 went on to bowl games but lost, taking some of the excitement away from the '59 season. Darwin (my baby brother) was born in 1961 completing our family with all four sons' first names starting with the letter D. We were Dan, David, Donald and Darwin; I guess my parents had a flair for alliteration.

Then came 1963 and the year that changed the community and school forever. It started out ominously when the main school building burned down because of old wiring and some defect in the building. Many who lived in the community for decades were heartbroken at the loss of the old school that had many memories in it.

The auxiliary buildings were not burned down; some being used as makeshift classrooms and even the Baptist church housed several of the grade school classes that year.

The school along with the football team refused to be dampened in their expectations by the mishap of the school burning down. The team continued to practice after losing their school building; the gym and field house received no damage. Because of these factors, the team gave the community something to remember that healed the loss of the school building.

The fifth year was Daddy's best one of his head coaching experience at Agricola, although the season began with a scoreless tie against St. John (a Catholic school on the Mississippi Gulf Coast). With all the commotion of losing the main school building and moving classes to cramped buildings, the team got off to a sloppy start. It rained constantly throughout the game making playing conditions unbearable and difficult to find any sure footing. However, the team afterwards ran the table winning the next eight games in dominating fashion. They finished with 8 wins and 1 tie for the only undefeated season of Daddy's coaching career. The height of the season featured the team beating archrivals Rocky Creek 33-0 for the first and last time.

The awards ceremony for the new Pascagoula River Conference was held in the Agricola gym, on November 22, 1963 and was the high point of Daddy's coaching career. The season had started with a tie that many blamed on a lack of preparation for the season because of scurrying around to get the school going with the building housing most of the classes burned down. None of the games after the tie, though, were even close and the Agricola powerhouse allowed only 13 points all season long by two teams. This achievement alone must have been some sort of record, making their defense almost impossible to score against. The offense on the other side was so explosive they blew everyone out and teams were finished off early.

Mike Wade the starting fullback was the Most Valuable Player of the league, with Daddy as the Coach of the Year for the Pascagoula River Conference. The day and afternoon ceremony were quickly dampened by the assassination of President Kennedy in Dallas. We heard about the tragedy immediately after the awards ceremony that made both events a contrast of joy and sorrow. The '63 team was one for the ages and the season seemed to stand out in time, making the year the most exciting time in Agricola during all the years I lived there.

The year that followed that golden year featured the schools of Agricola and Rocky Creek consolidating with Lucedale, forming George County High School for the 9th through the 12th grades. My Dad did a very noble thing: instead of moving our family out of Agricola, he chose to keep our family in the community.

Daddy agreed to coach the 7th and 8th grade football, basketball and baseball teams. I was on those teams and my 8th grade teams are ones I will always remember. I played one more year of junior high football at George County then turned to High School Baseball, which gave me a lot more opportunities because of my size. I was small but quick and really had not grown as much as I wished when I got to high school, so I got knocked around pretty good in football. However, I played on the Agricola teams and had Daddy as a coach in the 8th grade. My position was wide receiver and I was able to make some clutch catches during the season.

We played our archrivals, Rocky Creek and the rivalry continued even in the lower grades. Although we lost our first game against our nemesis that season we played them again and, we were really up for the second against the bulldogs. I helped win the game catching a touchdown pass in the first half and setting up another score with another longer catch in the second half. I will never forget the game with Daddy as my coach and the game's winning passes. This game was the highlight of my short football career and was especially rewarding because it was against our archrivals which we weren't able to beat in high school ball until the final season.

Daddy stayed on in Agricola to coach the 7th and 8th grade team one more year after I entered the big world of George County High School. I resented going there because I had pictured going to our little school in Agricola and loved the stage where my Dad was the head football coach. My dreams were not to be though, as reality set in and I played one more year of football in George County Junior High School, mostly sitting on the bench. Afterwards, I turned to baseball as my consuming passion and discovered I could do better in a sport that seemed to be more suited for me than football. I played all three years on the high school team batting .317 in my junior year.

David, (the oldest of my younger brothers) was still in the fifth grade when the people from East Central High School in the adjoining county came looking for Daddy as their new head football coach. Coach Charles McMullan, (Daddy's former assistant coach) was now coaching at East Central High School. Several Sunday afternoons, he visited my Dad and convinced him he could still live in Agricola and commute to East Central while coaching and teaching there at the school which was about 15 to 20 miles away. East Central had never been able to beat Agricola with the game in year 1963 billed as the clash of the two powerhouses going down as one of their biggest disappointments of a big game. When the big game came at the end of the season, it featured a 41-0 drubbing of the Hornets by the Agricola Warriors. The people responsible for getting a new coach knew of Daddy's coaching skills and they wanted a winning coach now. I remember Coach Mac (as we used to call him), watching us work out on our self-made baseball field. We marked off a field and put a backstop up to practice most of the time when we were not working. We spent many days there with Daddy throwing to us. Coach Mac said, "Dan could play on the high school baseball team." I never went with Daddy to the East Central School, which you could do back then at a specific school if it was where your parents taught, even if it was not in your district. My brother David went to East Central after attending George County one year while Donald went there and played mostly football. They did better competing at a smaller school like East Central because it was still in the old Pascagoula River Conference than they probably would have done at George County High

School. My youngest brother Darwin went to George County High School the way I did.

So, the Coach Nelson era begin at East Central in 1966. The supply of talent again was not very large, but as usual, Daddy got the most out of his teams than probably anybody could ever get. He had small players for the most part, so he designed the team for speed with the first year team demonstrating potential in 1966 and also showing marked improvement in 1967. The '67 team won the Pascagoula River Conference title for the first time in the school's history posting a record of 5-3-1.

Daddy was great at working with whatever coaching material he had and developing the strengths of every player progressively. He would usually bring out the best in every player through his coaching and outlook on them as potentially great players. The year 1968 featured many star players on the team including Quarterback Alan Goff, who after high school football at East Central went on to play at the University of Southern Mississippi with a scholarship as a defensive secondary back. Mike Long, (a tiny but fast back) set records in yardage and touchdowns while ends Ronald Kirkwood and Rodney Walker caught everything Goff pitched their way. Later most of these guys showed up at Mississippi Gulf Coast Jr. College, where I attended and graduated. I had the habit of saying things without thinking of what I was saying. Once I told them introducing myself, since I had gone to another high school, "I'm Coach Nelson's boy." Ronald Kirkwood never let me forget those words. Every time he saw me he would say, "That's Coach Nelson's boy."

The East Central team in 1968 set new scoring records, beating teams like Vancleave and O.L.V. (Our Lady of Victories) by over 50 points, with the victory over O.L.V. coming in the Pascagoula River Conference Championship game. The '67 season had featured a budding offense coming to maturity against teams who were weak. East Central beat Leakesville that year 54-0. This victory was particularly rewarding because of Daddy's dismissal from the school as coach before he went to Agricola. He even had people come up to him the last half and say, "Don't run up the score on this team." You get an idea of the drive my Dad had when he replied, "They weren't letting up on me when they fired me with no place to go, having a family and a pregnant wife." The truth is his team's offense was so explosive in '67 and '68 you couldn't hold them back. The '68 team scored over 400 points in that golden season, which was highly unusual for Mississippi High School Football. Their team went the opposite direction with their offense than the '63 Agricola team who had the stingy defense which allowed only 13 points against them all season.

The only blemish on the '68 schedule was a loss to the Catholic school; St. Stanislaus in Bay St. Louis on the Mississippi Gulf Coast. Two punts were blocked in the last quarter by the St. Stanislaus team when someone missed their assignments, costing the Hornets a perfect season.

The team finished with a 9 win and 1 loss record, winning the Pascagoula River Conference and beating another Catholic school: Notre Dame of Biloxi, in the Pickle bowl played at Mississippi Gulf Coast Jr. College in Perkinston, Mississippi. The most explosive team Daddy ever coached finished the season and garnered a bowl win as the icing on the cake while achieving a 10 and 1 record. Our house filled with plaques and honors on the wall, became a veritable museum. The two team pictures of the '68 Hornet team and '63 Warrior team along with footballs signed by the teams were some of the best memorabilia in the house, because they were most unforgettable and competitive teams. One other player that made the '68 East Central Hornets the perfect team was Terrance Wells, the first black player to be on the team. He and another black player broke the color barrier. Terrance's starring on the team was not without hazards, despite his ability as the best blocking back Daddy every coached. He could have scored a lot more touchdowns with a different coaching scheme. He scored some, but primarily mowed

down people and cleared the way for speedy smaller backs like
Mike Long. Some boosters though tried to intimidate Daddy not
to play Terrance. He had threats if he started Terrance, but Daddy
did not listen to them. He played the best players and no one was
as tough a player as Terrance when it came to blocking and running
over people. Terrance went on to the University of Southern
Mississippi to star there and was drafted by the Houston Oilers, also
playing for the Green Bay Packers. While I was a student at New
Orleans Baptist Seminary my brother David and his wife Brenda
went with my wife Janice and I for a game in the Superdome to
see Terrance start as running back for the Packers against the New
Orleans Saints. Terrance (now called Terry), played the whole game
and had some good plays and blocks. Such was the kind of player
Daddy gave a chance to play on his team, indicating Mississippi
football was changing. Black players were now playing and starting
on once segregated teams of all white players.

Terrance visited Daddy when his health was deteriorating and
participated in the funeral service as an Assistant Pastor of a church
in Jackson County. His presence and words were a great blessing
to the whole family. When I had a hard time finishing the funeral
sermon, Terrance gave me a handkerchief with his initials on it to
wipe the tears away, which he let me keep and I still treasure to this
day.

The peak time for East Central football was the '68 season.
Daddy retired from coaching after that season, despite coming
back for one more season in 1971, permanently retiring after that
year. Daddy coached my brother David in his junior year of the '71
season when the team finished with a 4-5-1 record. Ronnie Pierce,
my Dad's star quarterback at Agricola in the undefeated season
followed him as coach in the '72 season when my brother David
was a Senior.

After Daddy finally retired from coaching, he went into the
counseling field at the high school and later moved to the junior

high school at East Central. My brothers, David and Donald, finished high school at East Central because Daddy continued teaching there. Donald went on to star at Mississippi Gulf Coast Jr. College and later played football at Mississippi State University. He was on the team in 1980 that broke Alabama's long winning streak under Bear Bryant.

Donald went on to coach at several high schools in Alabama winning a state championship at Plantersville. Darwin finished high school at George County, playing more baseball (like me), and returned to coach at George County as an assistant for years. Both he and his wife retired early to embark on a singing career, performing at many types of venues. David, the brother next to me in age, worked for many years at various shipyards in the area and has served on the school board of the George County Public School System. I became a pastor, having completed 45 years recently since my ordination. The last 33 years I have served as Pastor of the First Baptist Church of Camarillo, California, in Southern California. The coaching legacy of my Dad continues through his sons and even David and I have done some coaching over the years. We have both coached Little League baseball and girls' softball. I coached the teams my daughters played on and am currently an instructor in Indoor Cycling, which is not quite team coaching, however it is instruction of a sport/activity at local gyms in our area.

4.

MASTER MOTIVATOR AND OTHER INTERESTING STORIES

After giving an overview of Daddy's coaching career, here we focus on the stories about him and those in our family. Some of these stories do not involve my Dad directly, but are included because he was either in the middle of them or to the side as an attentive observer and his influence can be seen in all these stories. The stories involve his early years, up to his retirement. This chapter grew considerably when I enlisted the help of my brothers who had many more stories to contribute; the chapter expanding exponentially from the initial first draft since everyone had their stories about Daddy. For quick reference, I have subtitled the stories and numbered them.

Locker Room Talks and Other Football Stuff

(1) The Half-Time Ignoring of the Team at Leakesville

In the fall of 1956, the Leakesville team was not performing up to expectations against the Richton Rebels. Behind at half-time 7 to 6, assignments had been missed and tackling was sloppy. Instead of a patented half-time speech, Coach Brooks Tisdale and Daddy engaged in a conversation on the best fishing and hunting places in Greene County. Daddy told Brooks where he was going to hunt for Thanksgiving vacation and so the banter went in front of the entire team, as they completely ignored the team. When the team was ready to go back out, one of the leaders said, "Coach, aren't you going to say anything to the team?" I think it was Tisdale who said, "Why should we, you haven't listened to anything we've said so far during the game. So why should we waste any time trying to talk to you?" That did it. The team got mad, went out, scored twice, winning the game 19 to 7.

(2) Whoever Misses the Next Block is going to Wear that Diaper

Since my Mother and Daddy had met in Runnelstown, they knew a lot of people there. So, when Agricola played Runnelstown in 1958, a lot of people who knew them came out. The Warriors were not cooperating in making Daddy's return back to Runnelstown a success. The team was behind 12 to 7 at halftime and Daddy was extremely frustrated, to the point where he got upset and lost it with the team. My mother had a baby bag for my brother Donald who she carried with her while she was close by my Dad and the team. The team huddled either outside or under the bleachers, not having a fieldhouse to rest in. With my mother close by, Daddy said, "Irma Lois give me that baby bag!" She gave the bag to Daddy as she listened to him chew out the team while unrolling a diaper from the bag. He said, "Next half I want to see somebody hit somebody and stop playing like babies." He continued, "The next block I see missed you are going to wear this diaper. The next person who misses a tackle that player is going to suck on this baby bottle (lifting it up for all to see). If you're going to play like babies, you ought to look like them." The fearful team went back, scored twice and won the game 19 to 12. They were ever-mindful that somebody might have to wear a diaper or suck on a baby bottle from half-time on. The threat served as a powerful motivator that led to a sweet victory.

(3) "I Don't Know How to Wear an Athletic Supporter"

Life was simple and plain for those country boys in Agricola who Daddy tried to mold into a football team his first and second season as coach. He had 20 or so players that first season. Some were not that familiar with football uniforms and the various other accessories that go with them. They found out really quick what some of these accessories were, even though they knew little about them beforehand.

One of Daddy's early players was a special young man who eventually wound up as equipment manager. He actually became a better equipment manager than player. He went out the first season, though, never having played before and had to acquaint himself with the parts of a football uniform and pads, which knowledge he later turned into a science as the equipment manager. The puzzled first time player had never seen an athletic supporter, so he asked another player (who was always on the mischievous side), "how do you wear this?" The experienced player said, "It's an extra guard for your nose."

Most of the team was already on the field practicing early when the young man ran out with a jock strap over his nose. The old helmet he was issued didn't have a face guard (or if it did it, was a single bar) so you could see the jock strap over his nose very clearly. Many will remember the old football field in Agricola. The field house was in the gym, so the football field was a good 500 ft. away from the dressing room. You could see the football players come out of the field house from a far distance. You can imagine the young man bursting out of the field house running to the field with the jock strap over his nose. What a sight to see; only in Agricola and back then in those old-school days.

Many had a hard time standing, they were bent over backward with laughter. Daddy had a hard time getting practice started again and he was right there with everyone side-splitting in merriment at this scene. The young man wasn't so trusting after that and found a better position as an equipment manager. He really found out what an athletic supporter was after such a trick played on him.

(4) The Mother of All Post-Game Pep Talks

The last game of Daddy's first season in 1958 at Agricola featured the chance of having a winning record at 6 wins and 4 losses or to wind up 5-5 with a loss. Agricola traveled to St. John Catholic School on the coast with it only being Agricola's second football season. Country schools had a reputation as being backward, so the St. John's team was standing around when the Agricola team filed off the bus, carrying their equipment in "burlap" sacks. The laughter was universal on the St. John's side. Name calling such as "country bumpkins," "hayseeds," and "backwoods" filled the air but Daddy saw real possibilities in their ridicule of his team.

Before the game, Daddy went into his Knute Rockne mode in the locker room. He said, "Did you hear them ridiculing you out there? They called you all kinds of names, thinking you don't know what you're doing out there on the football field." He continued, "Are you going to take that off them? Are you going to let them think you are all they said you were when you leave here tonight or do you have something to prove? Can you go out there and show them they will be ashamed for calling you "hayseeds", "country bumpkins", and "backwoods?" St. John had already won the conference and I believe had lost only one game. They were no match for Agricola that night however. Benny Shows ran wild and Agricola finished their second season with a winning mark of 6 and 4, embarrassing the St. John's Eagles 31-10. No longer did they have to win the respect of the St. John Eagles when they came to town.

(5) The Race to McClain with Brother Felty

Agricola was so small that Daddy coached all the football teams. We used to call the 7th and 8th grade teams "Pee Wees". Since money was limited, they had visiting games and initially couldn't afford to take the bus to their away games. They had to improvise and take the vehicles at hand in traveling to the away

Pee Wee games. This particular Saturday morning was tough because we had our 59 Corvair and Preacher Felty's station wagon to fit the entire team in. I was too young to play, but went anyway. Unbelievably, we had about 17 people between the two cars. Maybe some people went earlier to McClain, but I can't remember. To make matters worse, Preacher Felty and my Dad decided to have a race to McClain. Now it was only a short stretch on the bridge at the Leaf River, there was not any real danger and it was surely not a Nascar race. On a good day, you could get the Corvair up to 75 miles per hour and the preacher had an old station wagon which also, didn't have that much get up and go. With the cars bulging with passengers, it made the car race even slower. The slow pace of the cars did not dampen the spirits of the players in both cars. I think our Corvair pulled past the preacher's station wagon at the end of the bridge. When we won the game later on, however, it was almost anti-climactic to the race and the shouts of the boys in the cars.

The game was interesting in its own right, for when we got to the big metropolis of McClain they made fun of our team because some of us wore blue jeans since there was not enough football pants to go around. However, we beat them by about three touchdowns and no one was making fun of us when we left. Those blue jean-clad, bare-foot, leather helmeted boys put a whipping on cocky McClain. The player scoring the last winning touchdown trotted slowly by their bench which now at that point was almost dead silent. The slow strut past the losing team's bench may have been the origin of "the Deon Sanders strut."

The Pee Wee teams played with the cast off leather helmets from the high school team. Half the high school team used the old leather helmets during the first season. These were passed on to the Pee Wee team and I think they hung around for over a decade. Actually, when you were hit with those helmets they didn't hurt as bad as the hard ones. Daddy's Pee Wee teams always had a lot of drive and hustle.

(6) Handling the 6th Grade Class Rowdies Ronnie Pierce and Phillip Thompson

Ronnie Pierce, who visited with Daddy a couple of days before he died, told this story. Ronnie told of the way my Mother and Daddy worked in collusion regarding him and Lonnie Brannan, who were the class pills. Ronnie and Lonnie were very active in class and were quite a handful as big old boys for 6th graders. They also got bored really quickly and cut up a lot. My Mother told them, "My husband just started a Pee Wee football team for 7th and 8th graders. Since you boys are pretty big, maybe you can go to the afternoon practice."

She was trying to find an outlet, (or shall we say a cure) for their rowdiness. I wasn't around for the conversation but it may have been something like this: "Lorie, that Ronnie Pierce and Lonnie Brannon are a handful. It's really hard to have them all day and get them to pay any attention because their attention span is gone by the afternoon." He probably replied, "Send them down to me for football practice and we'll see how tough they are."

They went in the locker room and the sparse uniforms and equipment had already been issued so my Daddy made them practice without any pads. Even though they were big boys, they got beat up pretty bad. They came back after two or three weeks and determined they would be team players in my Mother's class. The daily beating in practice cured them of a lot of their rowdiness. They really were a lot better in class after their short stint at trying out for the football team. Ronnie got better though and was the quarterback on the 1963 undefeated championship football team. He wound up as one of the stars of that great team doing well, as did Lonnie. It really wasn't cruelty that they had no pads, it was just the way things were because the cupboard was bare when it came to cast-off football equipment for the Pee Wees.

(7) Daddy and the Boxing Match Challenge with a Player

Not everyone was interested in Daddy's work ethic the first year in Agricola. One player didn't think too highly of Daddy challenging him. He wondered why he should jump every time Daddy said jump. He didn't have to do what he didn't want to do, or so he thought. Daddy tried to let him know who was in charge. The player didn't want to follow what he said, but one day Daddy said, "You want to settle this? We will do it after school." Daddy had a pair of gloves that he saved for students wanting to fight. The player didn't know Daddy had some boxing savvy while serving in the Navy. They were all ready to go when my mother found out about it and lectured my Dad about behaving like a kid. My soon to be Step-Granddaddy, (who was the janitor) found out about it and finding my Mother cried, "They're going to fight, they're going to fight." At the last-minute the fight was called off but the player fell in line when he saw Daddy was serious and became a valuable player as well as becoming a close friend of the family for decades. He knew how far Daddy was willing to go had he refused to back down in order to achieve discipline on the team.

(8) The Old Triple Reverse with the Help of the Mosquito Truck

We were playing a Catholic school; Our Lady of Victories (OLV), at Pascagoula in 7th and 8th grade football. Mosquitoes are thick on the coast and a mosquito truck was spraying clouds of pesticide on the field. I was playing in that game off and on and we weren't moving the ball much down the field.

Daddy waited till the right moment when the pesticide cloud settled over the field, and then he called for a triple reverse. He thought the cloud and all types of ball-switching would fake everybody out. The play didn't score but it was a big pickup. He also had to rehearse who would get the ball, because he had never run the play before. Daddy's creativity in this situation showed the length he would go to win a football game.

(9) Meeting Paul (Bear) Bryant

My brothers and I grew up in the Paul (Bear) Bryant era of Alabama Football. We saw Joe Namath excel and many National Championships as the Crimson Tide owned the Southeastern Conference in the '60s.

We went to a Mobile A's Minor League Baseball game in the late 60s' with all kinds of future stars on the A's (like Rick Monday, Joe Rudi, Gene Tennace, and Blue Moon Odom). Bear Bryant came to the game and sat down in front of us. My Dad went down, getting on one knee to talk with him at his seat. He told him who he was and Bear treated him like a colleague. Daddy greatly admired Bear and patterned much of his coaching style after him. It was a rare moment that I'll never forget because we loved "the Bear." We never missed any of Alabama's game replay highlights with Bear.

(10) The Infamous Locker Room Throw-Outs

Although Daddy was a stern disciplinarian, he allowed a lot of levity inside the locker room. One of the rites of initiation was when a player was coming out of the shower or had stripped off his pads, the players would gang up on him and throw him outside in the buff. Then they would proceed to lock the door and the initiate had to run around to the front door, with the scene usually witnessed by someone. This practice became a norm and was a source of some interesting and revealing events. They never could get Mike Wade, (The Most Valuable Player of the Pascagoula River Conference in 1963) out the door. He was so tough not even a gang could weaken him. The rite was greatly curtailed when one of the players was pitched out right in front of one of the most pristine teachers in the school. She complained to the principal and the infamous throw-outs were practically all but shut down.

(11) Starting a Winning Tradition against Brett Favre's Dad's School

Brett Favre's Dad (Irvin) started coaching at Hancock North Central High School shortly after Daddy retired from coaching at East Central High School in 1972. The winning tradition of East Central continued with the team having a winning record against Hancock North Central. My brother David caught the winning pass against the team Brett Favre's Dad coached in 1972 when Ronnie Pierce, (the star quarterback for Agricola in their '63 undefeated season) succeeded my Dad as Head Coach of East Central High School. David also played under Daddy in 1971, when they defeated Hancock North Central 26-12 for Daddy's last game as a high school football coach.

A little 8-year-old boy was throwing perfect spirals behind Hancock North Central's bench in one of the games later that decade. Someone said, "That little boy throws well. If he keeps it up, he might play in college." Someone else said, "That's Brett, the coach's son." He made it well beyond college, to the pros and recently the Hall of Fame.

(12) Cheese and the Broken Leg

Jimmy Vise came from one of those families that had settled Agricola. His family was in the dairy business and his Dad, Devoe, was quite a character. Devoe always wanted you to come talk to him on the front porch when I picked up our family's newspaper the delivery person would throw out in front of his house. Our house like others at that time, did not have a personal house address so we picked our newspaper up at the Vise's house, getting to know them quite well.

Jimmy got the nickname, "Cheese." Because they had a photographer shooting his picture and someone hollered "say cheese." He could also fill those holes on defense. He had a handshake that was solid from milking cows all his life and it was one of the sternest handshakes I ever encountered. It was like putting your hand in a vice grip.

Jimmy was so tough that he broke his leg in the first half of a game and would not come out. I don't think he knew his leg was broken, I can't remember, but he managed to finish the game on the broken leg. He came back to finish the season a few games later playing with his crippled leg.

Oh, what players Daddy had! Much different, I must say (polar opposites), from what you see paraded in front of you today; players who really don't care much about teams, but rather their ego. You might say that's a negative reaction, but it's the truth. Bring back the players of that era that were team players all the way and found ways to sacrifice for the team the way Jimmy did.

(13) The Wrong Ending to the Game

The second season Daddy coached at Agricola featured vast improvement from his first season as coach. Agricola played their archrivals, the Rocky Creek Bulldogs, in a chance to play in the Singing River Conference Championship. Everything was on the line for the conference championship. The game was played at fever pitch displaying a hard-fought defensive battle, with both teams playing so well that it was very difficult to score. Agricola did manage to score a touchdown and held on for an apparent victory which would be the biggest in the history of the school. We had no electronic scoreboard and the referees called the game saying it was over.

The band was poised and began playing the victory march. People raced on to the field. We had done it! For the first time, we had beaten our archrivals. However, another referee called everyone back and announced there were about five seconds left in the game. The initial call for the ending of the game by the first referee was supposedly incorrect.

Rocky Creek had the ball on the 50-yard line with time for only a desperation pass. They threw up a "Hail Mary" and a bulldog caught it, slipping behind a defender. Rocky Creek scored the extra point and won 7 to 6.

We were stunned! One moment there was victory; the next, bitter defeat, all within a blink of an eye. What was especially painful was that Daddy said we must win this game or he would lose his job. It turns out Daddy was trying to motivate himself more than anyone else, which he did quite often. He did keep on coaching at Agricola after this memorable loss.

Of all the games in my Dad's coaching career that stand out, I remember this game the most because of the way we seemingly had won it and then lost it within a matter of minutes. Today, we would have called for a replay. Many believed the referees robbed us, especially after they had called the game initially.

Daddy was retained as the coach after Agricola won the Camellia Bowl in Lucedale (the county seat of George County). The contest was Agricola's first bowl game ever in this inaugural event for George County, which awarded a deserving team in the county with a bowl game. Daddy's team beat Richton 32-12 and finished with a 9-2 record. The presentation of the Camellia Bowl trophy by Sam Loftin Sr. was given to Daddy and the team. The picture of this event is on the back cover of this book. It was the first ever bowl game Agricola won. The season was a remarkable one considering it was only the school's third football season. Although Agricola won the Camellia Bowl that year, it was the season of the near miss and what could have been because of losing the disputed game to Rocky Creek.

(14) P.W. Underwood as Santa

P.W. Underwood was Rocky Creek's head coach in the infamous 1959 7-6 game. He coached several seasons in George County and went on to The University of Southern Mississippi, where he eventually became head football coach. Both P.W. and Daddy were good-natured rivals. After we got beat at the last second 7-6 and lost the conference title, I thought Daddy would be fired and wrongly thought that it was all P.W.'s fault.

P.W. so happened to play Santa Claus, being a big guy, at the annual county Christmas parade. When I realized who it was, I told everyone, "That's not Santa Claus! It's P.W. Underwood!" When he came down the street to our place, I tried to trip Santa up and I failed but brought a chuckle from P W. who just laughed at me and went on. It was the only time I tried to trip Santa and it was also the last time, for afterwards Daddy had a pretty intense and appropriate reprimand with me, (if you know what I mean).

(15) Too Much Hype for Rocky Creek

The Agricola team got better within a couple of more years and it brought a fever pitch of emotions which arose against our archrival; Rocky Creek. We had two or three pep rallies. Grade-schoolers were given placards saying, "We'll chop off their tails, and box in their ears." Everyone was confident we'd win this one, but they don't play the game in pep rallies. The first play was a kickoff for a touchdown that Rocky Creek ran back immediately. It went downhill from there and we got beat 32-14. Next year however, we finally broke through with the 33-0 win even without a lot of fanfare. All the hype didn't work to beat our archrivals, but playing good football does secure victories.

(16) One more Rocky Creek Story I figured in Prominently

The year that followed that golden year of an undefeated championship featured the schools of Agricola and Rocky Creek consolidating with Lucedale, forming George County High School for 9th through 12th grades. My Dad did a very noble thing by not leaving Agricola and choosing to stay in the community. He thought it was better not to move his family out of Agricola.

My Dad instead agreed to coach the 7th and 8th grade football, basketball, and baseball teams. I was on those teams and my 8th grade football team is one I will never forget. I played one more year of Jr. High football at George County, after which I just played High School Baseball. David and Donald went on to East Central High School and played there.

The rivalry with Rocky Creek continued in football after losing our first game with them, we played a second game, which was our homecoming game. I was a wide-receiver and the secondary wasn't covering me well. I snuck through the secondary the first half and caught a touchdown pass from our quarterback: Darwin Allen. The second half I caught another long pass on a halfback option from Brad Broadus setting up the winning score. It was the highlight of my short football career and was especially rewarding because it was against our archrivals. I caught a long pass in the same way a Rocky Creek player did to win the disputed game in 1959. It was refreshing that I had scored in similar fashion Rocky Creek had won the earlier disputed high school football game in '59.

(17) Barefoot Football Players

I remember the Pee Wee football team at Agricola for many reasons, but generally because they were short on everything. Farm boys sometimes didn't even have any sneakers. If you were lucky, you could buy PF Flyer sneakers or Converse tennis shoes to play the games. You had to furnish your own footwear and when you didn't have any, you couldn't play in boots, so you just went barefooted.

It wasn't a rarity to see Daddy's Pee Wee teams with various assortments of footwear. In high school, we marveled at Arthur Hatcher's 15 triple E shoe size; a big old tackle whose shoe seemed almost as big as Shaquille O'Neils' shoes. The Pee Wees would have barefoot boys playing into November. It didn't seem to bother them and often the best players on the team played barefooted.

(18) When Name Calling Worked

I don't know if Daddy gave nicknames to people but there seemed to be a bunch of them. Jimmy Vise was "Cheese," Clifton Taylor was "Fred Flintstone" or "Flintrock" because he was a hard man to block off the board drill. Jimmy Davis, the fullback, was "Foots" noted for his moves. There were many other nicknames. Daddy would especially call somebody a well-chosen name or use it in a phrase for extra motivation, like: "You're blocking like a girl!" or "I've seen better tackling by old people!" Every time he used these phrases, they were designed to get the most out of the team.

Jimmy (Foots) Davis always fascinated Daddy with him hailing from a little place south of Agricola called Movella, (a little spot outside Agricola, just before the Jackson county line). Each summer his family would go to state/county fairs and carnivals, spending most of their time up north in Wisconsin, Michigan, and Minnesota. They operated a concession stand they would pull with them all over these states. Nicknamed "Foots" because of his prowess in running a football, as I remember, he was a good blocker too. He not only ran through holes in the line, he opened them up.

(19) Confidence While Coaching

Daddy got his team to believe in themselves. Several times he would draw the play they were going to run then send it over to the opposing coach saying, "This is the play we're going to run and you can't stop us from scoring." Usually, they didn't stop them either with his team's explosive offense.

(20) The Board and Pit Drill

Daddy really stressed blocking in football and followed Vince Lombardi's style for executing plays with everybody carrying out assignments. Two drills he practiced over and over again were "the board drill" and "the pit drill." He would do match-ups to see who could move somebody down the board. The "pit drill" was conducted in the high jump sawdust pit. You tried to get out and the other fellow tried to stop you. Clifton Taylor excelled in all these drills as well as Mike Wade. These were guys you couldn't move on the board or stop from getting out of the pit. When fights broke out in scrimmage, players were just moved over to these drills. It wasn't just another day at the office or football field, there was something new every day.

(21) Give the Ball to Me

My Dad being the coach had some perks in getting into game situations. In 7th grade, I didn't play first string but got in for some plays. We were losing to East Central with about 15 seconds left in the game and trailing by about 10 points, so Daddy said, "Go in and tell them to give you the ball for the extra point." I told the quarterback to give the ball to me. He was sort of amazed since I had not been playing much in the game.

The quarterback did give me the ball and a hole opened up for an extra point that I went through but standing at the goal was a guy who was going to level me. I went down before we collided and got ragged all the way back home on the bus by some lineman who said. "We had the hole opened and you chickened out." Having a coach for a Dad has advantages but it also has drawbacks.

(22) Country Hicks can Play Pretty Well

There was a perceived notion that small country places were a little backward and were pushovers. After five years at Agricola, Daddy proved that assumption wrong. The final year of truth was the perception that you were in for a hard-fought game when you played Agricola. Given a lot of offensive stuff, Daddy threw at you in Agricola and later East Central, his teams overpowered you instead of it being the other way around.

(23) McClain's Cheers Were Short-Lived

In 1963, Agricola rolled into McClain highly favored to do what they had done to most opponents: to soundly beat almost every team they played that year. Daddy's ideal team would always put the game away early. McClain had a pretty decent team that year and their hopes were bolstered when they returned the opening kickoff for a touchdown. I was coming out of the visitors' locker room, late for some reason and heard a great roar go up from the McClain faithful when they scored. They really thought they could beat us and the opening kickoff return for a touchdown served as their short-lived reason for false hope. It all changed, when Agricola quickly scored twice and wore them down by the first half to win by about 40 or so points.

(24) The Lowest Points Allowed by Any Team

The mighty Agricola Warriors team of 1963 only allowed 13 points. They scored 248 points on offense and allowed 7 points to State Line and 6 points to McClain in the opening kickoff, which I described in the previous story. This defensive domination must be some kind of record that may never be breeched. The kickoff return for a touchdown by McClain resulted in Agricola coming back to win in their highest offensive output of 48 points against any team. The touchdown State Line scored against Agricola was sort of a charity give away. They would have had a scoreless season if it had not been for these two blemishes.

There may be another team somewhere, which was that stingy with points allowed, but there could only be a select few. The harsh reality of any games they played was: You were not going to score against Agricola, no matter what you did!

Agricola would put the game away early on offense then not allow any points. It made them one of the most feared teams of the 1963 High School Football season in the state of Mississippi. It was by far Daddy's best defensive team. My brother Donald pointed out these facts, having been a defensive coordinator and coaching high school teams as head coach specializing in defense himself.

(25) A Literal New Team at Halftime

The Vancleave Bulldogs cheated when our 7th and 8th grade teams played them in one game at Agricola. They rolled out some high school players who suited up to play us in Agricola's high school football team's undefeated season of 1963. Running up the score and beating us badly the first half, prompted Buddy Howard, our coach to do something different.

The difference amounted to our Junior Varsity team, switching uniforms with some of us 7th graders when we came out of the locker room starting the 3rd quarter. Surely, Vancleave noticed our team was bigger but couldn't do anything about it.

Our team came back and begin to score with David Gunter a 9th or 10th grader as our quarterback. However, Vancleave ran up the score so bad the first half we didn't win. We started out as a 7th and 8th grade game and ended up as a Junior Varsity game. It was very noticeable with a new quarterback, new running backs, linemen and receivers.

The next year we traveled to Vancleave they did the same thing, playing high school players again. Vancleave still had a high school but Agricola didn't have one because of consolidation of the smaller high schools into one central one in Lucedale. We were really taking our medicine and couldn't do the same thing we had done the year before by using high school players, especially with an away game. Mercifully, there came a deluge and the referees called the 4th quarter off.

The original game, with the switch of the players the year before was one of the weirdest football games I ever saw played. The Jr. Varsity team took over the second half and from the size of Vancleave's players we were glad to let them do it.

(26) The Epic Game didn't live up to its Expectations

It was billed as the most important game in each school's history. The East Central Hornets, where Daddy coached three years later, were headed for a collision course with the mighty Agricola Warriors in their undefeated season. The Hornets were the young upstarts of the Pascagoula River Conference going undefeated up until their next to the last game of the season with Agricola. Agricola had known winning football under Daddy, but nothing like this season with their undefeated season and stingy defense. The teams would meet to decide the winner of the Pascagoula River Conference.

East Central featured a fast offense with Benny Goff as quarterback and Mike Jones as the starting running back. Their defense was not sloppy either, although not as stingy as Agricola's defense. They rolled into Agricola expecting an undefeated season and a conference championship. However, they had to beat Agricola, which was a tall order.

Daddy had drilled the team hard in practice and he wanted this game and the conference championship. Something had to give and everyone was expecting a tight game that would go down to the wire. I pictured shades of the Agricola/Rocky Creek game four years earlier when someone would win on a last second pass.

No one was prepared for what actually happened. The game was pretty tight the first quarter and into the second, then Agricola's offensive game came alive. Long runs and passes were the rule of the day and Mike Wade, the star fullback, could not be stopped.

Agricola put the game away and it was no contest. When Mike Holifield (a new transfer player from Moss Point and a speedster), returned a punt for an 80-yard touchdown, the game became a laugher. Agricola demolished East Central 41-0. Such was the strength of Agricola's team that Holifield couldn't even crack the starting lineup, even though he had started for bigger schools in bigger conferences. Daddy used him wisely as a decoy, pass receiver out of the backfield and punt returner.

I supported some of my Daddy's psychology when I talked with Roland Bufkin, who was a great Agricola running back. Early in the season, I joked with him saying, "Holifield is coming and he could take your place in the backfield." He skinned my head because my remarks were a little troubling to Roland but he never wavered having an ideal season and doing great in the backfield with Jimmy "Foots" Davis who also had a magnificent season. They were a running back tandem that no one could stop. Mike Wade was moved from the line to fullback and the team scored at will, especially against East Central.

I was in the locker room the next week as Daddy's team was preparing for the final game with Vancleave and Holifield's run was shown. The team stood collectively and cheered. They knew no one could beat them and that they were the best team in the conference. What was supposed to be a nail-biter turned into a rout. Agricola beat Vancleave the next week in a sort of lack-luster performance winning 20-0, but still allowing no points to finish undefeated that year in the last year of Agricola High School football and the end of an era.

(27) Motivational Examples of Daddy's Coaching

Ronnie Pierce, Daddy's starting quarterback on the undefeated Agricola High School Football Team gave a couple of examples of how his old coach used motivation in his coaching.

Ronnie revealed, "Coach Nelson had the gift of motivation." He related how in football practice the team could see our family's house from the practice field. If the practice wasn't going well, Daddy would say, "You are going to cause me to lose that house, my kids go hungry and have to move." Ronnie said, "We couldn't let that happen."

In 1963 Daddy's team played probably the biggest game in Agricola High School or George County history. Agricola and East Central were both undefeated and clashed for the Pascagoula River Conference Championship.

Agricola's starting quarterback shared how Daddy orchestrated a Friday night like no team had ever experienced: "First, we were told not to go home after lunch, which we always did. We went to the gym, laid on the floor and asked no questions. At 4:30 p.m., we were told to go to the cafeteria. There the mothers of the players had a pre-game meal. We had never heard of a pre-game meal. At 6:30 p.m., we were ready to take the field." Daddy pulled out a very large chalkboard. On the chalkboard were all the starting team and the East Central players they were opposing. Written below the Agricola players were the parents name of each boy. The pep talk theme was this: "Are you going to disappoint these parents?" Ronnie said, "I have never played with or coached with such and inspired group of players." The final score was Agricola 41-East Central 0.

(28) Daddy handpicked his Successor as Head Coach of East Central High School when he retired for the Final Time.

Daddy believed Ronnie Pierce, his starting quarterback for the undefeated 1963 Agricola Football Team should succeed him as Head Coach of East Central High School. His former quarterback shared his most lasting memory of his relationship with my Dad. Daddy retired for the last time in 1971 and Ronnie served as an assistant coach on the East Central team in his final year. He shared how his old coach sat him down and informed him he was going to retire for good. My Dad told his assistant coach that he would be the head coach. Ronnie said, " I'm only 24 years old." Daddy replied, "Age has nothing to do with it. It's knowledge, effort, will and heart that will make you a good coach. I've raised you and I'm not a failure, so you will not be a failure either." Ronnie shared how Coach Nelson still inspires him after all these years and still has an impact on so many people by his influence in the early years of their lives.

ABOVE is the famous undefeated team of 1963 that made it all happen. These were great players in a dream season. They gave up only 13 points all season long and won the Pascagoula River Conference that year undisputed. Daddy was awarded the *Coach of the Year* for the Conference.

This is the famous East Central Team of 1968 who won the Pascagoula River Conference and the Pickle Bowl. Several players went on to college from this team. They were explosive in their offense scoring over 400 points that season.

TOP: Jimmy Vise

RIGHT: Daddy's famous pose as a High School football coach

BELOW: Deacon Dozier Rogers

Coaches, clippings, scores and Mike Wade
of '63 undefeated team

SEASON'S SCOREBOARD

Team	We	They
St. John	0	0
State Line	38	7
O. L. V.	20	0
Beat Four	32	0
Rocky Creek	32	0
McLain	48	0
D'Iberville	20	0
East Central	41	0
Vancleave	27	0

WARRIOR COACHES

Mike Wade
Outstanding Back, P. R. C.

ABOVE: Earlier picture of the brothers

BELOW: Pee Wee team picture 1963, with me as the
first player on the left in the first row.

Unforgettable Agricola Characters

(1) Stop Tommy from Guarding Me

My Dad was always trying to help the underdog. Tommy Parker was a young man with special challenges who probably would have been in a special needs class today. He was highly animated and often mumbled to himself. Despite these difficulties, he tried out for the basketball team and was a sight to see. He ran like the tin man on the Wizard of Oz, which was definitely noticeable on the basketball court.

All the sports teams at Agricola High and Jr. High were coached by Daddy and Charles McMullan. Coach Mac coached the boys and girls high school basketball teams and my Dad coached the 7th and 8th grade basketball teams.

Agricola was beating a bad team; a small 7th and 8th grade team from Tanner-Williams located just inside the Alabama state line. There was a little time left on the clock, so it was time for Tommy and the reserves. David Gunter, a starter, stayed on the floor to anchor the last couple of minutes with the other reserves. After a few plays, David called time out and went over to Daddy frantically saying, "Coach Nelson, I think it's commendable what you're trying to do by letting Tommy play, but could you tell him to stop guarding me!"

(2) Bobby Thompson: Deputy Sheriff

Bobby Thompson was about a 300 lb. guy it seemed that looked as big as a bear. Bobby lay down on the floor and talked with us, looking like a real bear rug one day, when Daddy and I were shampooing Bobby's carpet, (Daddy's side job he had during the summer).

Bobby regularly ran for sheriff and lost often. Once Bobby promised a group of people a lot of stuff at a political rally; when he was elected sheriff he would make this and that happen. Daddy said,

"Bobby, you're really going to do all that?" Bobby said, "Well, you have to tell those people something to satisfy them."

Bobby had three big boys: Rex, Phillip, and Robert, who all played football for Daddy's teams at Agricola. Bobby used to tell Daddy, "My big old boys were right in the thick of all your winning."

Once, Daddy and the men dressed up like country women during a benefit for something or another at the school. Daddy came out with a flower dress, a big bonnet, and a corn-cob pipe playing his guitar with Lester Williams, who was quite a character in his own right. Suddenly, Lester was terrified of something in the audience and couldn't go on with his song. Daddy asked, "What's wrong?" Lester said, "That man's got a double-barreled shotgun pointed right at me!" Daddy said, "Don't worry, that's only Bobby Thompson's nose!"

(3) Mr. Elmo Bunch, the Green-Keeper

Elmo Bunch was a committed Christian and served faithfully at Agricola Baptist Church. He was also a green-keeper at the George County Golf Course for many years there. He was so ingrained due to his longstanding position there on the golf course that his ashes were actually scattered on the sixth hole. When you got to that spot during a round of golf you were always close to Mr. Bunch as you played the course. Daddy was a good friend of Mr. Bunch and saw a lot of him on the golf course, always carrying on extended conversations with him as a regular fixture at the golf course.

Mr. Elmo always told little truisms as modern day proverbs. He once told my brother Donald, "The biggest room is not the Astrodome or the Superdome, but "the room for improvement." Boy, is that a wise maximum!

Once there were three fellows who started playing on the golf course without paying their green fees. Mr. Bunch confronted them and told them they had not paid their green fees. One man said, "Who's going to make us pay?" Mr. Bunch replied, "I didn't spend four years in the U.S. Marines for nothing!" This thinly veiled threat resulted in the men promptly paying their green fees.

Having played several rounds of golf at the George County Golf Course, I was surprised in my recent trip to learn it had been shut down and put up for sale. My brother Darwin who was the Golf Coach at George County High School and coached two state championship teams told me the sad story of trying to get it going again. I hope for a number of reasons; (Mr. Bunch being one of them), that a plan can be carried out to buy it and renovate it. It seems a shame after so many years devoted by Mr. Bunch and having state championship teams with no course to play on should result in its present unkept condition. I hope someone or some group can do something soon for the longstanding George County Golf Course.

(4) Crafton Parker's Haircutting Adventure

We had a first-class barbershop in Agricola. Crafton Parker, an old army barber, walled off a section of his porch and used to charge 50¢ a pop for a haircut. We usually got the standard army haircut, which looked like you had a bowl put over the top of your head and everything else was cut close, if not shaved. Then Crafton would put a little butch pomade on the front part of your head. Daddy used to let all of us wrestle to see who got a haircut first every time we went to his barbershop. You may think I have a lot of stories, but you should have heard Crafton.

He was hard-of-hearing from a hunting accident and had a different story every time we visited him for a haircut. He could tell you something about the family background of everybody in Agricola. Sometimes Daddy would bring his guitar and play while we got sheared, which was quiet an experience. The extras related to getting a haircut at Crafton Parkers' barbershop made it a fun experience.

Crafton always had a wad of tobacco in his mouth and would not spit next to him but rather across the way in a makeshift spittoon. He was a short little fellow and the wad of tobacco in his mouth was almost as big as him, or so it seemed. Many-a-time I've heard that jet-stream of spittle go directly under my earlobe. He always aimed straight, though, and never hit me (for which I am very thankful).

(5) Mr. Dozier: What do you want to hit me for?

A lifelong buddy of Crafton's was Deacon Dozier Rogers. Dozier actually had his ear partially bit off by Crafton when they were boys. A doctor sewed it back on, but Mr. Dozer had a scar on his ear the rest of his life because of this tussle with Crafton as a young man. Mr. Dozier was a deacon for 54 years at Agricola Baptist Church. He became our Grandpa when he married our grandmother after she became a widow. We noticed he took a long time taking the hog slop to the pigs we had at our house and he stayed around the house courting my grandmother.

Mr. Dozier loved Tommy Parker and Tommy used to say, "That Mr. Dozier, he's crazy!" Mr. Dozier would give you the shirt off his back and was the long-time janitor at the Agricola School, holding that job for decades. A godly man, he loved everybody no matter what they did to him and he trusted everyone, much to his chagrin. He was really grateful to God when I became a preacher, as he had prayed for someone in his family to be called by the Lord as a preacher.

I can't begin to describe the impact Mr. Dozier had on my life. He was a man of prayer and I saw him go into his bedroom once and not come out till God gave him an answer about his grandson, Charles, recovering after a near fatal auto accident.

Mr. Dozier had more faith than many preachers. Once during a dry summer, he reminded the preacher at the time to pray for rain; prompting the preacher to say, "Oh Mr. Rogers, you and your prayers."

He was a soul-winner and shared the gospel with people in almost any situation. I have seen him sit in a doctor's office and ask almost everyone where they went to church and if they were saved. He picked up hitchhikers and witnessed to them. He witnessed to Mr. Dee Parker who didn't have much time for what Mr. Dozier had to say to him. The situation changed however, with Mr. Dee having a heart attack landing him in the hospital. Dee told him, "Mr. Rogers, I've asked myself, many times the question you asked me the other day when I didn't want you to talk with me: "Are you born-again?" Mr. Dozier led Dee to trust Christ as His Saviour there in the local hospital.

Mr. Dozier actually died witnessing to a man and praying for him to find Christ. Denny Baker had been in a bad car accident and was in critical condition. Mr. Dozier said he was ready to go be with the Lord so he asked God to take him and spare Denny, so that he would have another opportunity to be saved. He prayed earnestly for Denny to live so he could be saved. Denny lived and trusted Christ while Mr. Dozier, (who was in the hospital with heart problems) died shortly afterwards.

Mr. Dozier used to go forward and pray at the front for souls. I have never seen anyone so burdened as much as he was for the lost and no one who had hardly any formal education be such an effective witness.

Mr. Dozier's favorite preacher was Billy Sunday who he heard in person once on a trip to Chicago. He said, "Dan, sometimes you preach like him." Maybe more accurate was the way I used to roam on the stage the way Sunday did.

I have spent many hours in the little house his son Herman built for Mr. Dozier and my Grandmother. We would talk about the deep things of God in the Bible. We would pray, discuss how good

God is, what He wanted to do in my life and what he had done in Mr. Dozier's life. When he passed on, I mourned for him as I did my own Daddy, but I know that soul-winning drive I saw in him has been passed on to me. Much more could be said of this wonderful man and there are many funny stories. The following story is one of the ones I remember the most.

We had a touch-football game going most of the time during the football season. One day, we enlisted Mr. Dozier to be a receiver. Daddy said, "You run this pattern and I'll hit you." Mr. Dozier asked, "What do you want to hit me for? I haven't done anything to you! I'm not aiming to start a fight!" Such was the banter we had with Mr. Dozier.

(6) Devoe Vise and the Front Porch

Mr. DeVoe Vise was Jimmy Vise's Dad. They maintained a dairy that had been in the family for what seemed like forever. We did not have a street address during the time I grew up in Agricola. In recent decades, the address of 134 Fire Dept. Road was assigned to our house.

We got the Mississippi Press Register, but they could not deliver it to a place that did not have an address. The person delivering the newspaper would throw it out at Mr. Devoe's house about a mile south of Agricola proper. I, being the only son with a driver's license was designated to drive the car to get the paper. Mr. Devoe and some of the family would usually be out on the front porch by about 5 PM. By that time milking was over for the day and I knew this was an arduous journey every time, but I also enjoyed driving the car.

You see, when Mr. Devoe saw me pick up the paper, he would holler, "Boy, come on over here and talk to me," and began to ask me something along the lines: "What are you studying in school? How is your team doing? How is your family?" Mr. Devoe would always have a story about Mr. Dozier (my Grandpa), or Daddy. A short trip to pick up the paper resulted in a 45-minute conversation with Mr. Devoe on the front porch. My mother didn't have to ask why I took so long to return home. She would just say, "I can see Mr. Devoe got you to talk to him again."

After several years, my resentment turned into appreciation for the time spent talking with Mr.Devoe on the front porch. Mike Hunter, a former neighbor down the way once said, "He gets the Mr. Hospitality award hands down." During my teenage years, I was only focused on sports and had an inferiority complex while Mr. DeVoe made me talk to him.

When I went on to college and seminary, he would hear me preach at my home church occasionally. Mr. Devoe would always tell my mother, "I was the one who got that boy out of his shell." I did learn a lot about the history of Agricola, about Mr. Dozier, (since Mr.Devoe and him were buddies) and I learned everything about the school. I also learned it is good to be folksy with people in the church, the way Mr. DeVoe was. Mr. Devoe knew everyone since he had been on the school board and never ran out of stories to tell or questions to ask you.

(7) Hack Gunter and the Explosion

There was a farmer (Hack Gunter), who had a lot of land in Agricola, and he had quite a temper. He was considered as a deacon at one time, but a fellow deacon said, "I heard Mr. Hack drive the cattle home last night and I don't think he'd be too good deacon material right now, maybe we'd better hold off for a while."

Hack's son David was the hardest working boy I have ever seen. At 12, he was out plowing a tractor into the night with a light on. No one worked harder than David did. He was a model of hard work for everyone his age. I picked up pecans, helped plant soybeans, and loaded watermelons for Mr. Hack while I was growing up. When I stopped to breathe one time, while picking up roots out of newly broken land, he said, "If you want to play with the birds or loaf, I'll send you home right now."

Once, a Little League baseball team from Chickasaw, Alabama, (out of Mobile) came to Agricola and kept catcalling Mr. Hack, who was umpiring the game. I knew something was going to happen when I saw Hack turn beet red under the umpire's mask, then go after the coach prompting Daddy and several others to pull them apart. Someone else finished umpiring the game, but that sure livened up the game. I think they trounced us but the tussle was worth the price of admission, (which was free).

I must say that Hack transferred all that emotion into his work and was the hardest worker I ever met. He also made you work and spent long hours in the fields. Later (if he did not sell it cheaply), he donated the land where the Agricola Baptist church new additions are and their softball fields stand today. Hack Gunter stands out as another one of those unforgettable characters in Agricola

(8) Danny Walters "Frog Man"

Danny Walters was a strange kid in my class and would do anything on a dare. He was noted for folding his eyelids up giving him a frog look so much that the girls would scream when they saw him.

He was on the kickoff team for 7th and 8th grade and Scott Tanner, (our punter) used to kick the ball really high but not very far. Danny would be on the end and would catch the ball before the punt returner could and started running it back. We had to flag Danny down several times and tell him, "You can't do that."

Many people thought Danny was a little wild, but he proved himself a hero rescuing soldiers he served with in Vietnam, coming back a decorated hero. No one laughed at him after that heroic event and his courageous service.

(9) The Airplane Pilot's Mask and Eugene Wall

Eugene Wall was quite a piece of work, always kidding around and wise-cracking with a lot of people. He had spent some time in California and eventually moved there. He would play practical jokes on my friends in Boy Scouts, but also became an easy target for jokes on himself.

Ghost stories around the campfire were the order of the day in Boy Scouts and usually someone got a little fearful after the story. One night, Daddy told of an airplane which had crashed in the near vicinity and they had never found the pilot. Eugene had really teased many people on this camping trip and it was now time to get him back. Daddy gave somebody an airplane pilot's mask, and in about 30 minutes things had settled down and the lights went out. Someone rolled into Eugene's tent with the mask on fully embracing him. Eugene jumped up, hollered, and high-tailed it out of camp. They had to run him down, catch him and tell him it was only a joke.

(10) Paul Bullard: The Whistler

Paul Bullard was our next-door neighbor for many years. He and his wife Aileen were mainstays in the Agricola community and the Agricola Baptist Church. They raised three daughters and settled down to retire after putting in many decades of teaching. Mr. Bullard was the Principal of Agricola Elementary School after it was consolidated, staying in the community the way my parents did. He was a tall person who always made his presence known by whistling around the house while working.

Mr. Bullard and Daddy were hunting buddies and even had bird dogs who were brothers, although we got the best of the deal there. Don, our dog was a superb bird dog who would always hold a point. Joe, his dog, flushed many a covey, so Mr. Bullard got an electronic dog collar to shock him when he ran into the birds and did not stop and point where they were.

Mr. Bullard was a deacon and Gideon speaking in my first church for me. He told me about his trip across the West when I planned to go to California and attend school there. Sometimes, he would come out and pitch baseballs as well as field with us and was one of the greatest neighbors you could ever have, along with the Browns up the road. His family was part of the group of houses, together where everyone was a teacher and we called "Teachersville."

Mr. Bullard was a good friend to the pastors at Agricola Baptist Church. His closest pastor friend was probably Lawrence Baylot, but he had a difficulty going with him hunting and fishing. One time while fishing, he hooked Brother Baylot in the mouth or close to it. Hunting turned out to be no better. When he went hunting with Brother Baylot, his gun went off accidentally winging the preacher in the foot. Once while fishing with waders, the pastor wandered out with Mr. Bullard and almost disappeared in a step off. Brother Baylot and Mr. Bullard stopped going fishing and hunting for the preacher's survival. The standing joke was you did not want to go hunting or fishing with Mr. Bullard if you were a preacher, he would get you by accident if not by design.

Mr. Bullard was a rock solid self-made man who always had a project going on in the garden, fly shop, building something or doing just about anything. Daddy saved his life once when he had a heart attack and rushed him to the hospital in time for life-saving medical attention. The day he died and went on to be with the Lord we lost one of the best neighbors anyone could ever ask for. When I visited all the way from California I halfway expected to hear that whistle in the yard over there, letting me know he was busy with something but now he's doing it in heaven. I wrote a poem to mark the occasion: "No More Whistling in the Bullard's Yard" (See Appendix 4). We miss him, but will see him again, accident free, in a joyous reunion of next door neighbors.

(11) Roger Dale Pierce and the Backstop

We constructed a baseball field with a pitcher's mound and backstop which Daddy helped us build. It was a great place to practice, although we ran out of room on the right field line. When we hit it out of the park the nearby soybean fields would hide the ball. I would have a quick temper if I couldn't find the ball.

Immediately after coming home after school many times I would throw balls at the backstop off the pitcher's mound and from the shortstop position. I became so identifiable that in trying to give a man directions to our house, he said, "Is that the home where the boy is out there throwing baseballs all the time."

Usually I worked out for an hour or more a lot of times till it was dusk. About the time, I was ready to go into the house most evenings, Roger Dale Pierce would stop his truck at our house on his way home from work. He was a big old boy that Daddy had coached on most of his teams at Agricola.

Roger Dale lived down the road and he had this musical voice which was sort of slurry, with a squint in his eye. He would tell me, "Let me throw some to you." Boy, did he throw the ball hard and wild. He put all his weight behind each pitch and really lugged them up there grunting when he pitched. It made me a little fearful the first few times because he was so wild and it was getting dark. He would say, "Stay in there against me." I did learn to hang in there against his fast pitching. Roger Dale was quite a character who really helped me hit a fast ball. The fast-pitching neighbor up the road, passed away not long ago and Agricola is missing quite a character with his death. He was never too tired to throw me a few pitches. My impromptu practice, was a great example of what it is like living where you know folks and they know you.

(12) The Hello World Crowd

The only service station in Agricola when I was growing up was initially called *Hello World Service Station*. Frank Tolbert was its first owner, who was a spinner of tall tales himself. Eventually, the Pierce brothers became owners and usually knew everyone who came in. Most of the Pierce families lived down the road and Daddy coached many of them and the people who worked at the service station for them. You could pump you own gas and tell them to put it on your bill or they would pump the gas for you at no extra charge. My brother, Donald, told me to go by there at about 6 a.m. in the morning (when I was back once on vacation from California), if I wanted to hear some stories and rub shoulders with some of these characters who gathered to talk and tell tall tales. I went down there a few times and though the coffee wasn't the greatest in the world, stories were tall and reminiscent of the Hee Haw gang. Everyone joined in with stories and information about people in the community. It seemed to be the center of the universe there in Agricola and was a great place to learn about country people in the community where we grew up.

School and Scout Stories

(1) The Pitfalls of being Around Our Parents All the Time at School

I never resented my parents as my own teachers and rather enjoyed it at times. My mother taught me in the 4th grade (as she did all my brothers), and my Dad was my teacher in 7th and 8th grade. Although, there were some pitfalls with my parents being my teachers and attending a small school, where everyone knew what was happening with everyone. My mother constantly had somebody coming to her and saying, "Mrs. Nelson, do you know what your son Dan said or did?"

The tipping point came one day in 5th grade when some boys were teasing a girl with a doll. I went one step further to outdo all the other boys, taking her doll and throwing it down. I didn't break it but at about the same time I was doing this, my Dad came around the corner and witnessed the whole incident, incriminating me in his full view. He just motioned for me to come to him and I knew exactly what was coming next. We went around the corner to the locker room and then he took the paddle down with holes in it. I took my wallet out and he burned up my behind, making me apologize to the girl whose doll I had thrown down. I promised never to do something like that again and I never did.

I never was out of my parent's sight (or so it seemed). I look back on their being around me all the time as a good motivation. I lived with the reality that I had better behave myself because they were always watching. However, I was never upset they were there because I needed watching and they did a thorough job of keeping track of their sons.

(2) The Belt Line

Daddy was also my scoutmaster and kept strict discipline with Troop 122. The way he did it was by a method that probably would not be acceptable today. When someone misbehaved, the guilty party was designated by Daddy to run through the belt line. Everyone took their belts off and whacked you as you ran through the line. All the boys got their turn to whack the offender on the rear. One trip through the gauntlet led to that boy listening and obeying well. Believe me, I know by personal experience it leads to behaving right.

(3) Surprise, Surprise, Surprise at an Old Friend's House

Our family was traveling from Jackson back to Agricola on Highway 49, which is between Jackson and Hattiesburg, Mississippi when we decided to visit old friends of my parents, who they had taught with in the past. My parents always tried to stay in touch with these old-time friends who meant so much to them. We stopped in with the whole family to surprise them and boy was it a surprise! Our ages ranged from about 12 to 3 at the time. We all had to use the bathroom and the husband told us there was one in the back, not knowing his wife was dressing there. We ran down the hall, opened the door, and was surprised to see an over 60-year-old woman in her bra and girdle getting ready. She made the best of it and acted just as normal as anything, but it caused us to run away quicker than we came in and after this surprise experience. We didn't have to go to the bathroom all that bad after all.

(4) Tab Sure Does Weird Things to You

As I mentioned, Daddy sort of stumbled into coaching football. Certainly, he was familiar with it and going to Mississippi Southern gave him an even greater appreciation of football. He was a novice though and T.T. Murphree, the principal he followed, kept encouraging him in the Moselle, Leakesville, then Agricola schools. After Agricola, Mr. Murphree went into administration in several school districts. Daddy maintained a life-long friendship with Mr. Murphree and it seemed like Daddy followed Mr. Murphree wherever he went, since they were such good friends. Jimmy Vise, a lifetime friend, told this story at Daddy's retirement roast about his friendship with Mr. Murphree (although it really doesn't sound true). It seems T.T. Murphree was trying to recruit Daddy for the third time to follow him and coach at Agricola.

Daddy and T.T. Murprhee were on a train and someone poured Tab, (that early diet drink that tasted awful). Daddy drank his Tab first as the train went through a tunnel. Daddy stopped Mr. Murphree from drinking the accursed soft drink and said, "Don't drink that, Mr. Murphree, it makes you go blind when you drink it!"

(5) Daddy Occupying a Chair on His Favorite Teacher's Page

Daddy was a real people person, but he accumulated a few enemies along the way. More people by far loved him than didn't, and whenever there was someone who didn't like him it was usually a straight-laced teacher who didn't care for his kidding with the students. One such teacher was someone who had to be in control and have everything just right with her class at the school.

I can't remember if Daddy was still coaching or had gone into counseling at East Central when this incident took place, but many of the students were aware of the dislike this teacher had for my Dad. Some way, some students in her organization had taken a picture of him sitting on a toilet seat in the back of a truck, "fully clothed." The yearbook staff got hold of the picture and promptly displayed it in "the thinker statue" pose on the controlling teachers' organization page. Can you imagine the shock of the teacher when she opened the copy of her brand-new yearbook with that picture on her page of Daddy in his famous pose for all time and memorial? It probably cemented her dislike for him.

(6) Getting Students Involved

Daddy laid out a physical fitness course in the days of the "President's Council on Physical Fitness." His course was featured on the front page of the weekly paper. He also told everybody when they completed it a helicopter was going to come to this very spot. He arranged for an army recruiter to come, escorted by the helicopter to that very place on the course laid out by the students.

Once Daddy told his classes he needed a golf cart and he didn't have enough money for one. They pitched in and helped collect enough cans and bottles until one day he finally had enough to buy one. It also kept the campus a lot cleaner, demonstrating a method to his madness.

(7) Fights and Recesses

Buddy Howard was Daddy's assistant coach the year of the conference championship of 1963 and was assigned to playground detail for 5th through 8th grades when he coached the Pee Wee team. Fights seemed to break out with regularity on the playground, so he did something I'm sure you couldn't do today. Each day, a couple of guys paired up, put on boxing gloves, and duked it out. I got the best of Richard "Rabbit" Pierce but Rusty Bedgood got the best of me, although the consolation to the loser was the girls had pity on you. Such were the days of the playground boxing matches; I am sure never to be repeated again.

(8) Daddy's Boast in Counseling

Daddy retired from coaching and moved into school counseling before he completely retired. His famous statement about his counseling staff was, "I can't say we are the best counseling group in the world, but we started out with a monkey at the beginning of the year and he ended up a brain surgeon at the end of the year."

(9) A People Greeter at Wal-Mart

The last job Daddy had after school was that of a people greeter at Wal-Mart in the county seat of Lucedale. He saw the people he had coached and taught through the decades, making it the perfect retirement job for him. His former students got to see Coach Nelson again where he told their children about their parents.

(10) Missing Jake Morgan on the Field Trip

Daddy took Scout Troop 122 to old Brookley Field in Mobile, Alabama, to see all the airplanes at the Air Force Base. Mothers were chaperoning the group, but Jake Morgan was missing when it was time to go, leading to a massive manhunt. What had been an enjoyable trip turned into total panic, so four hours later they went home (unable to locate Jake), only to learn that he had left with an aunt earlier without telling anyone. Jake had been at home, safe the whole time as everyone else were in a frenzy trying to find the lost boy. The buddy system didn't work too well in this situation.

(11) Floor Hockey with a Dust Mop

Improvising was part of Boy Scouts with one of the most challenging games in gym: floor hockey, featured throwing a shirt down and two participants with dust mops tried to push it across the foul-line first. The game was not as easy as it looked and a struggle usually ensued.

Floor Hockey was a good spectator sport, especially if the score was close. The scouts got excited and cheered their teams on. The game was a favorite of the scout troop and one of the many multi-faceted games Daddy always had planned for Boy Scouts.

(12) The Old Agricola School Burns Down

On a hot summer night, a few weeks before the opening of school in the fall of 1963, Lutheree Hamilton woke our family up when she drove her car into our driveway. I ran outside and saw tears in her eyes as she cried, "That's what's left of the Agricola School burning down." We saw a fireball in the distance and with the fire, Agricola changed forever. The student population was consolidated into a county high school in another year. Gone were the days of a little school and knowing everything about everyone. My Dad would not be the Head Football coach of the high school I would attend, leading to a big disappointment I never got over.

The community and school pulled together, (as already stated in the previous chapter) and the last year of Agricola High School was their best football season ever.

A redeeming factor that I have used as a sermon illustration was the effect of the Agricola School fire. Everything burned to a crisp the next day and everyone toured the burned down school. We went over to the trophy case and most of the trophies were melted except for one. Although, covered with soot, the big round basketball trophy the Agricola girls' team won for the state championship in 1956 was still intact. The surviving trophy is like the works that we do for the Lord, to be tried with all Christians at what is called the Judgment Seat of Christ in I Corinthians 3:13. It says, "The fire will try every man's work of what sort it is."[2] Gold will not burn but only be enhanced as demonstrated by the solid gold trophy the girls had won. It served as a fitting reminder of victory in the midst of trials to our faith.

(13) Injurious Situations at the Old School and Football Field

I was either clumsy or just prone to accidents, which led to several mishaps growing up as a boy. Two accidents that were caused in the old school were shocking and brought sudden pain. The day after our old school at Agricola burned down in 1963, we were trying to find salvageable stuff by sifting through the pile of rubble. Several of us boys started picking up pieces of broken bricks and sailing them. One rock I picked up tore my finger when I pitched it, causing profuse bleeding, and I was rushed to the doctor's office. It took five stitches to sew my finger back together. I still have a scar to this day because of that fateful incident. When I came out stitched up, I remember my Step-Grandad Mr. Dozier Rogers, (who accompanied my Dad and I to the Doctor's office) asking everyone there if they went to church and trying to witness to them in the waiting room. He never gave up sharing His faith and enjoyed it.

The second injury came when we were visiting with someone at the football field that was right behind the old dilapidated house

---

2 All Scriptural quotations taken from the King James Version of the Bible unless otherwise indicated.

we lived in for a while, before we moved to our new one. We called it the "rat house" and lived there on the campus for a time meaning we were at school all the time. We were with some people showing them the football field that was rustic with the seats of solid concrete. The press box, (if you could even call it that) was on the third tier of seats at the 50-yard line marker. I went up there with my shirt off on a hot August day and beat on the box not realizing that a large wasp nest was under it. They all came out, being awakened, and attached themselves immediately to my stomach. Daddy got me home and put an ice pack on my stomach because I really started hurting. Another trip to the Doctor was in order, who gave me several shots to reduce the swelling. I never beat on anything like that again without looking under it first.

Being at an older school in a rural area did have its pitfalls when it came to things you could get hurt on and it's a wonder I didn't get hurt worse. The old stuff that I played with does lead to unforgettable memories; however painful they might have been at the time.

(14) Political Rallies

We used to have political rallies at the old Agricola school and you could usually make a buck or two passing out cards for candidates. My parents backed Jack Tub (who I met in a rally he attended) for State Superintendent of Education. I remember putting one of his cards on each button of my shirt and a picture was taken of me with all his business cards on each button.

There were a lot of promises and hot air at these rallies where candidates got to speak and meet people. It was all natural to the flow of traditional southern politics and the politicians who ran for office.

(15) Civil War Studies

Daddy made history very interesting in his classes and especially made American history come alive. Specializing in the

Civil War, he got interested in it because a pastor had let him read his collection of Civil War books when he was a boy. My Dad would do things like ask the class to make scale models of the ironclad ships: The Monitor and the Merrimac.

I developed Daddy's interest in the Civil War starting with comic books, then going on to hard back books and others I would read for hours. Sometimes I would read the same books repeatedly. I couldn't get enough of all the battles and characters in the conflict.

We toured the Vicksburg battlefield close to my Grandparents house in Jackson, Mississippi, when we visited with them. We would also visit the retirement home of Jefferson Davis (the President of the Confederacy) called *Beauvoir* in Biloxi on the Mississippi Gulf Coast. All these trips were during the centennial observance of the Civil War when everything was at a fever pitch.

Our family discovered we had two Great-Great Granddaddies that had fought for the Confederacy. The knowledge of the Civil War served me well in school where I went on to have a Double Major at William Carey University in Biblical Studies and History.

One day while I was in the fifth grade, my Dad asked me to come in and ask questions to his 11th grade class in U.S History about the Civil War. They tried to stump me by asking questions they thought I did not know. They asked me which battle it was in which the Northern soldiers sewed names on their clothes so they could be identified when shot and killed in the battle. This group of soldiers resigned themselves to certain death through the hopelessness of the charges by the Northern army. Immediately I knew the answer was the Battle of Fredericksburg and the senseless charges made on Marye's Heights.

The question I asked the class that stumped them was: Who was the first person killed in the Civil War? No one was killed actually in the first day of the bombardment of Fort Sumter in Charleston, South Carolina on April 12, 1861. The next day however the Northern army evacuated Fort Sumter under Major Robert Anderson. A battery went off in a boat accidentally killing Private Daniel Hough, a Northern soldier who became the first casualty of the Civil War.[3] No one got the answer to my question and could not have without further research. Again, what I did in going into the classroom was something that would hardly be allowed today.

(16) The Oldest Mardi Gras in America is not in New Orleans

The oldest Mardi Gras in America was in Mobile, Alabama, which began in the 1700's with the coming of the French explorers.[4] It's revival was commonly believed to predate the Civil War and the New Orleans Mardi Gras origins. Usually, the Agricola High School band would play in one of the parades, leading to a fun field trip to Mobile only about 30 miles away. I remember seeing a local television station interviewing Agricola band members in one of the afternoon programs. It was really a big deal to see Agricola High school students on TV if you lived in Agricola.

The Mardi Gras in Mobile was much safer than the one in New Orleans. While going to seminary in New Orleans, we were warned not to go downtown on "Fat Tuesday." It was a wild place and you didn't have to worry about that type of environment with the Mardi Gras in Mobile being more of a family celebration where the kids could be on the streets without fear. We went once or twice to the one in Mobile. It is a little-known fact that the Mobile Mardi Gras predates the one in New Orleans.

---

3   Damian Shiels, Irish in the Civil War: Revealed: The Tipperary Town Where the First Soldier to Die in the American Civil War was Born? (Accessed August 14, 2016, https://irishamericancivilwar.com/2013/03/24/revealed-the-tipperary-town-where-the-first-soldier-to-die-in-the-american-civil-war-was-born/, March 24, 2013, New York, Herald Tribune.
4   David Harris, A History of Mardi Gras in Mobile, Alabama, http://traveltips.usatoday.com/history-mardi-gras-mobile-alabama-21559.html, (Accessed August 14, 2016), A History of Mardi Gras in Mobile, Alabama, USA Today.

(17) Cotina's Restaurant

There were no eating establishments in Agricola in the early 60's. I went to the high school games with Daddy on the bus as early as the 4th grade and would travel with the team. Many of the team's away games were against teams on the Mississippi Gulf Coast so we would usually stop late at Cotina's Restaurant in Pascagoula on our way back from a game.

Since the team did not have much of a meal before any of the away games, everyone chowed down after the contest. If the band traveled with us, then everyone went in mass to Cotina's after the game.

Cotina's always had a big banquet room and they majored in Greek cuisine since the owner was Greek. I had lamb for the first time there and the food was so good that Greek food is still one of my favorite foods to this very day. It was a great event to go to Cotina's for those after-the-game meals which I looked forward to almost as much as the games.

(18) The Coffee Pot Restaurant: A Classic

At the heart of Lucedale (our county seat) was The Coffee Pot Restaurant. It was at the main intersection of one of our few red lights and we often went there for after-the-game meals.

The Coffee Pot had quite a reputation and was owned by the Bailey family who had operated it for years. They eventually sold the restaurant and it was remodeled into a Chinese restaurant.

Tennessee Ernie Ford was traveling through Lucedale one time and stopped at the Coffee Pot to eat. A reporter from the local paper down the street interviewed Ford concerning his menu choices. He was torn between the Hamburger Steak and the Fried Chicken because the food was so good; and it was hard to decide what to order.

There was also a classic landmark in front of the restaurant called Bailey's Scratching Post which had ridges on it and where you could scratch your back. Tennessee Ernie scratched his back on the post and a photographer for the local paper shot a picture of it and put it on the front page.

Lucedale would have a hospitality day once a year, featuring the local sheriff stopping someone with out-of-state plates and treating them to a free meal at the Coffee Pot Restaurant after giving them a key to the city.

I used to work at Smith's Grocery down the street and would have 45 minutes to eat lunch, with the service being very slow. I was barely able to order, eat and get back to work. They were always short on servers but the food was great and worth waiting for. The reputation of the Coffee Pot Restaurant was known throughout George County as well as the surrounding counties.

(19) Getting pulled out of the Pool Room by my Mother

The pool room in Lucedale, Mississippi was to the side of the Coffee Pot Restaurant. It had boards in the windows that covered half the window so no one could see what was happening inside there. There was gambling and older guys who smoked cigars inside which did not provide a good environment, although no alcohol was there because the county was dry. Pool rooms in those days, such as the one in George County were associated with more bad things than good things back then. The old adage I heard in church was "If you want to live above sin, live above a pool room."

My cousin Charles, wanted me to skip the last period one day in high school and go with him to the pool room, where I had not been before. I said, "I can't do that, my Mother doesn't want me to go there." He said, "She won't find out and it won't hurt anything." Reluctantly, I went over and started playing a non-gambling game with Charles.

Suddenly I heard a tap on the glass and there was my mother gazing into the room, with her eyes locked into my eyes like a laser beam. It was not a happy moment; she actually went in, and grabbed me either by the ear or by the shirt, giving me a lecture about being in that "bad place." She gave me strict orders to stay away from my cousin and I did for a while.

(20) It's Time to go Home from the Hospital

Daddy was seriously injured once playing in a softball game when a student kicked him in the leg. The player slid either into a base or home plate with sharp pointed boots. The accident caused a blood clot and hospitalized Daddy until they got the clot dissolved. We were concerned because it was a serious injury and his leg was very bruised with not much circulation; plus, there was the threat of the clot going to his brain.

He could not walk but eventually recovered in the hospital. Another friend was in the hospital, leading Daddy (always the competitor), to race with him up and down the halls of the George County Hospital in their wheel chairs. When the doctor got the report from the nurses of the races down the hall he said, "It's time for him to go home."

(21) Scouting and the Snakes with the Order of the Arrow:

The Boy Scouts had an organization dedicated to camping and patterned after the Native Americans. They would have a campfire where members would dance around and tap you out to be in the Order of the Arrow. You had to pass the ordeal for outdoor camping before being admitted to the group. I and others in our troop were initiated into the organization by this method. My Dad encouraged participation in the Order of the Arrow through his example and many camping trips we participated in with him as scoutmaster.

There were other times at camporees when many troops came together and the members danced with snakes. They had tape over the snake's mouth and they were common non-poisonous snakes, native to the area around the swamp surrounding the camping site there in Jackson County. Once we were talking with other scouts from the area while we were there, when suddenly an older scout came with one of the snakes wrapped around his arm. I kept my distance as we talked with the boy. The snake snipped at him and he slapped it down saying. "Stop that, he's always trying to bite me." His little tussle with the snake made me draw back from him even more.

I saw pock marks on the arm where the snake had bit him. The snake did not harm him, but we questioned his mentality to use it as a pet in the first place.

I used this memory as a sermon illustration about people having pet sins they don't think are hurting them. However, at closer inspection you will see the effects of sin on their lives, even though they are in denial about them.

I loved scouting and camping out but really didn't want to get that close to the inhabitants of the area, especially the snakes. Again, you would never see something like that happen today.

(22) Winning Ribbons and Camping out with Scouting

My Dad was a great scout leader because of his military experience and his love for the outdoors. We took home several ribbons for our troop in different contests such as signaling with a flag and building a fire to boil water contest. It was fun and exciting, making our scouting experience worthwhile. We also camped out as a troop, locally and it was fun sharing a tent with your Dad and getting away from civilization.

Later, I camped out with friends such as Kenny Counselman. Living in the country gave us abundant opportunities to camp out locally. Kenny's family lived further out in the country and I always enjoyed occasionally going home after church with him and camping out. Kenny loved camping so much that after he moved to Florida, he still went back to his old home and built a small one-room house to camp out with his wife, Jackie. He loved the outdoors and I feel sorry for boys and girls growing up now that never had the outdoor scouting and exploring activities that we had. City-dwellers would say we missed a lot by not having as many stores and venues around, but they missed out on the great outdoors and the opportunities it afforded right at our doorstep.

(23) Moving Quickly after coming face to face with Snakes

There were abundant opportunities to encounter snakes in the country. Occasionally, you would see someone stop the car after running over a rattlesnake and there would usually be another one around after that. The snakes seemed to travel in twos and you had to watch going into several areas around ponds, because the snakes would blend in with objects in the land. I walked carefully on the path to Dean's pond which was close to our house. A big old water moccasin could wrap around a stump and you could not see it until it opened its mouth and then you saw the white inside it which is why they were also known as "cottonmouths." I have seen a water moccasin as big around as a boa constrictor. It gets bigger every time I tell this story.

In the hot humid summer, we would go swimming and dive off bridges into the different swimming holes. We used to swim in the cold water of Cedar Creek and dive off the bridge there on the highway. Once, I jumped into the creek and in submerging saw and heard everyone on the bridge jumping up and down crying out that a snake just passed over the place I dove into. I moved as quick as I had ever moved getting out of the swimming hole, not giving the snake any chance to get me.

Another time, while fishing with my brother Donald, the boat we were in kept drifting in under the cypress trees. My brother suddenly said, "Watch out! There's a snake in the tree." I looked up and again came face to face with a snake. I didn't take time to determine what kind it was, but just made a back door to the boat really quick. You've got to watch out for those snakes or they will get you.

Family Stuff and Interests

(1) What a Woman to Stand by Her Man

My Mother, Irma Lois Nelson has not been mentioned much up to this point, but she was a remarkable woman. She taught grade school for 40 years and my brothers used to joke about who could get the most whippings from her. Donald won hands down, having the distinction of being the son with the most spankings. My Mother grew up on a farm in Runnelstown, Mississippi, where Daddy met her. She raised four boys; we wanted one more brother we joked, to have a basketball team. My Mother could lay down the law when need-be and was noted as a good teacher.

My Mother had a very loud voice, which you could hear over everybody else. You could hear her in her classroom when you walked into the elementary school where she taught. We would sweat and strain through the season with Daddy but when football season was over, there was always something else we did, like hunting or fishing. My mother would usually clean anything Daddy brought home although he would skin the fish.

Once, Daddy had been fishing and they were camping out somewhere. He didn't wash off after cleaning the fish properly and rolled into the tent only to get kicked back out. She said, "Wash yourself up before you come in here and get rid of that fish smell!"

(2) The Old Party Line

The Party Line is a bygone memory that today's youth know nothing about. Everyone shared the same phone line and were designated certain rings if the call was for your family. Our phone had three rings, signaling for us to pick up. Someone could pick up before you did though and they could listen in on your conversation. That's how everyone knew everything about everybody.

My Mother was a weekly columnist for the George County Times, reporting about people who visited people in the community and people who went on shopping trips to nearby Mobile. She gathered information each week from everyone and was on the phone a lot. She was the most likely candidate to run into the malady of the party line. I'm not saying my mother listened to others' conversations, but several times she had people pick up on her. You could tell when someone picked up on you, because they usually would take a breath or two and you knew they were listening to your conversation. On more than one occasion, I heard my mother talking with someone telling them, "Wait, just a second." Then she would holler in the phone: "WILL YOU GET OFF THE PHONE RIGHT NOW!" They usually would get off because she had a loud voice and I sort of take after her in that department.

Those party line days were quite hilarious and I'm sure the next generation is in wonderment as to why any such thing ever existed. It did exist however and people were a lot closer back then. I wonder if there could be a lesson here by the phone connection that people shared.

(3) The Out-of-Control Student Situation

The courage of my Dad was really tested when we moved to Agricola for the first year. A guy, who I think was a high school dropout student, was a problem. One day he got into his car with several rowdies and started speeding down the country roads of Agricola. He did wheelies in our driveway at the old Hamilton house that we were renting at the time.

Daddy's courage came to the forefront when he went out to talk with the boy creating the problem. He was greeted by the boy and his friends who got out of the car, with one holding an empty wine bottle. One look from the front window caused my mother to gasp and say, "What if he hits Daddy over the head?"

Daddy stood his ground and told the troublemakers that there were children in the house who could have been playing in the driveway. He told them, "You're not going to come here and put everybody in danger. If you come back, I'll call the sheriff and if you want to take me on, I'm ready." They got in the car and drove off and we never saw him again. Daddy put himself between us and harm that day and became a hero to our family.

That day I learned we had a Dad who protected us, because he was willing to put himself between danger and us. Jesus talked of being the Good Shepherd in John 10, who like a faithful shepherd put himself between wild animals or thieves there to destroy the sheepfold. In essence, that is what salvation is all about. Jesus took the penalty for sin on the cross by dying there for us. Through Christ's sacrifice, we can be saved and have eternal life if we trust Him. A perfect picture of Christ laying down His life was visualized that day when my Daddy was ready to lay down his life for our family.

(4) Donald and the Sit-Ups

Donald went further than any of the other brothers to play college football. He even won the "Guts Award" at Mississippi Gulf Coast Junior College for being the toughest player on the team. Daddy saw a football player in Donald early on and trained him to do sit-ups as a toddler, taking pride in showing all the relatives, coaches, and friends how he could do them. He was like a little trained monkey that my Dad could pull out and show off. It must have worked because Donald went on to become a great player and coach like Daddy.

In school once, Daddy demonstrated Donald's toughness when, after giving a deserved whipping to a student, he showed how Donald could take the same lick and not cry. Sure enough, Donald took it without a whimper.

(5) We Built It and They Came

Every Sunday after church, we had a flock of people; a bunch of friends related to all the brothers to play at our makeshift baseball/football field where we had a backstop. Daddy would sometimes come out and play with us in the middle of all the boys there. We usually played touch football in the fall and winter, then baseball throughout the spring and summer. Sometimes we had over 20 to 30 friends over and we played for at least a couple of hours. My mother would pop out with grape flavored Kool-Aid that she served to everyone, which made your lips purple. Our house was the place to be on Sunday afternoons because we were always playing some sport. We then went inside the house for the Alabama/Auburn replay shows of the college football game from the previous day. What a life it was when your Daddy was the head football coach and you knew everybody in the school and town.

(6) Me and My Brother David pretending Football, Basketball, and Baseball Games

I don't remember why I did it, but I memorized most of the team's rosters that I rooted for. Initially, my brother David and I played each other constantly. We had "Backyard Stadium" with a smaller fence where we played whiffle ball and we had "Country Side Ball Park" where we had imaginary games we played with longer fences. Donald and Darwin eventually played with us as they grew older. We would go through an entire game and pretend to have our own bowl games like the Christmas and Turkey Bowl. Why we did it, as I said, I do not recall. I guess we were so into sports that we never stopped thinking about it; everything we did reflected it.

We played Little League and other sports, then played pretend games when we weren't playing actual sporting events. Donald said that I would be broadcasting a game and a car would go by, then I would quickly get out of the mode until the car drove by. Daddy's competitive nature was so influential on us, that we even pretended to play when we weren't in actual games and he never felt that we had too much sports. Competitive sports kept us out of a lot of trouble.

I would even get into the old Ford Falcon, listening to WCKY and later WLW in Cincinnati to hear the Red's games. At the time it was the only radio that could get the station carrying the Reds games in Cincinnati. The Cincinnati Reds have been my favorite team and my favorite player was Pete Rose. I tried to play like him in high school baseball and on summer league baseball teams.

(7) David and the Bird Count

I think the best shot of any of my brothers was David. He shot many birds with his BB gun and later pellet gun. One year he had a count going of all the birds he shot. I do not know how many he shot, but I know it was a lot. You could always see him bringing another bird back to the house. He tied them together by their legs. David shot a lot of blue jays with only that BB and pellet gun. David's hunting prowess was a result of being raised in a home with a hunting enthusiast like our Dad.

(8) Uncle Carol—the Family Clown

Uncle Carol was Daddy's one and only brother who was younger, which resulted in them being very close. It all started when they were young. Their parents had saved up for one bike for a Christmas present that the two of them had to share along with Carol's twin sister, Carolyn.

Carolyn was the only daughter, so she got to ride the bike first on Christmas morning parking it at the general store behind a truck. The driver did not see it and backed over it, demolishing the bike. Incidents like that drew Daddy and Uncle Carol close, but they did not have that close a bond with their sister, who they thought was babied by our grandparents.

In high school, when a bully picked on Carol, Daddy told his brother, "If you don't fight him and beat him up, I'll beat you up."

After that, Carol whipped the bully and he gave his older brother all the credit. Carol followed his brother into the service, also serving in the Navy. After the war, the brothers learned to play the guitar together. We always went to visit Uncle Carol's family and our first cousins Jimmy and Laura, after Daddy and his brother were married and had families. Carol always thought highly of Daddy.

It's hard to explain about Uncle Carol and all of his comical characteristics. He could make you laugh when he came into a room and could imitate people like John Wayne, James Cagney and Jimmy Stewart. Uncle Carol and Daddy took turns being the housewife and salesman, practicing how to sell Electrolux vacuum cleaners, which was another occupation Daddy had primarily in the summer. Carol also pursued this line of work to supplement his United Gas job.

Carol was about the hairiest man I ever saw. When he had his shirt off, he looked like a monkey in his chest and he would tell us, that's what he got for hanging out with the monkeys. We loved Uncle Carol and he would come up with a nickname for everybody. He used to call Jimmy (his only son) "whistle britches." He was married to Willina Nelson, or "Willie" as we used to call her. I used to tell everyone that my aunt was "Willie Nelson." It seemed she was the nicest person on earth with her hospitality and kindness to others.

Uncle Carol used to shine when imitating our Great Uncle Sam. He would walk with a jakeleg the way Sam (Granddaddy's twin), used to do which was an effect of Sam drinking moonshine whiskey. You never knew what he was going to say next; he was so much fun to be around. Carol went to Daddy's funeral and passed on a few years ago. After Daddy's funeral, we all went back to the house, sharing stories about our colorful family. Uncle Carol would imitate Uncle Sam and whomever else we asked him to and it was entirely fitting that the day we said goodbye to Daddy, would end that way.

(9) Hit by a Line Drive

My Dad was always practicing sports with us and since I liked baseball best, I always remember him pitching to us. Donald smacked him right in the face with a line drive when he was throwing batting practice once. I thought Donald had killed Daddy, especially when the shot drew blood from his nose and he was lying pretty still on the ground. He got back up however, and resumed throwing, as if it was nothing. Daddy was tough and an incident like this one proved it.

(10) Uncle Sam

Uncle Sam was my Granddaddy's twin brother. We had his funeral on the 4th of July, (no kidding). I helped officiate a graveside service with the Presbyterian pastor who led Sam to Christ before he died. As I mentioned Sam was the black sheep of the family. He got jakeleg from making and consuming moonshine whiskey. Once while driving a car for the family, he couldn't get the Model-A started. As people became impatient, he grabbed the keys and threw them into the slough off the side of the road. No one carried a spare set then so everybody else got out and started searching furiously like chickens pecking, as they hunted for the keys. Boy, did he have a temper! Of course, that hasn't been passed down to us! Anyway, at his funeral, none of his children came to it and they did not have the service in the church. I don't know of everything he did but God forgave him at the end, if he trusted in Jesus as his Saviour the way the preacher said he did.

(11) J.P. Collingsworth's House

We used to visit relatives in Northern Louisiana and on the trip there Daddy would lead us in a car game of getting so many points for different kinds of cars we passed. We also had a running count on all the dead armadillos we saw. We used to stay a night or two in the Collingsworth's house in Danville, close to Jonesboro, Louisiana.

J.P. was my Granddaddy's half-brother, who lived at the end
of a remote country road. People who drove down that road were
either coming to see you or had headed in the wrong direction. I
could never sleep well when we were there because of all the army
surplus stuff in different rooms. You would think you saw ghosts in
the corners and it was too quiet as well. We used to play with our
cousin, Wanda, and we would sit on their front porch, which was
the longest I'd ever seen. It was an over 100-year-old house where
my Grandpa and Uncle Sam (his twin brother), had grown up.
On Saturday nights, back in the early 20's, they would go to town
and usually pay a dime to watch a movie in the theater. One other
thing that made J.P.'s house spooky was that you had to pass by a
graveyard that was close by to get to the house.

Daddy use to recall how Uncle Sam and my Granddaddy would
walk home on Saturday night about 11 p.m. When they passed by the
cemetery, they imagined unusual things that seemed real. They were
so scared, they would pull their hats down over their ears "tighter than
Dickie's hatband" as Daddy said, and run as fast as they could to the
house. Their little sprint past the graveyard would be great training
today for track and field.

(12) Singing River Don

Daddy loved hunting since he had learned to shoot for game
early as a boy with his father. At Leakesville, he loved to go
deer-hunting, but later in Agricola with all the soybean fields, he
switched over to hunting for Bob White Quail.

To find the birds, we always had bird dogs. Daddy's most
famous dog was a Riff-Raff Pointer officially named "Singing River
Don".

A great dog, Don would hold a point and his brother Joe was
our neighbor Mr. Paul Bullard's dog. Mr. Bullard could not cure Joe
of flushing coveys of quail even with an electric dog collar. He used
it on Joe but it didn't help much, because Joe could not spot the

quail like his brother. Don, though, would hold a point beautifully and Daddy killed many quail with his help. He had better instincts as a bird dog and was Daddy's greatest dog.

Don got bit by a rattlesnake once and Daddy rushed him to the vet who was able to save his life. We accused our Dad of loving his dog more than us. Don's reputation grew as a great hunting dog and Daddy loved hunting with him.

Several men wanted to breed Don with their dogs. One day a man with a pickup truck (who I had never seen before), pulled up and asked if he could breed his dog with Don. It took me a while to realize he wanted to do it now at the immediate moment. Daddy was gone so I said, "I guess so." The man promptly let his bird dog out and put her in the dog-pen with Don. A few minutes later, Daddy pulled up and the man (whom Daddy knew) said, "I asked your boy if I could breed my dog with yours and he said it was alright." Daddy looked over at the pen and said, "Looks like he's doing a pretty good job of it."

(13) Daddy was a Stern Disciplinarian

Daddy made us mind and carry out our responsibilities at home. We had an acre of land which meant a lot of grass mowing. I got the lion's share of the grass mowing. If Daddy told you to do something once and you didn't do it, you were in trouble. He didn't like telling you to do the same thing the second time. It was usually with his belt that he told you to do something again which he used for more than holding up his pants.

Once he told me to cut the yard but my favorite T.V. program: "Batman" was on. That was not good enough though, for Daddy because it was getting dark and he wanted it done. I went out there and got upset that I was missing my favorite program. So, I slammed the lawnmower down and decided to run off. All of a sudden I heard someone burning up the turf behind me. It was Daddy, who had come out the house like a rabbit but ran after me like a grizzly bear with a belt in his hand. He was bigger than me and I thought I could outrun him. I was wrong about that, because he caught me and gave me a whipping (which actually I needed since I did have a rebellious spirit). When we got to the house, it was dark and I thought at least I wouldn't have to mow the grass until the next day. I was wrong again in my assumption about it being too dark to cut the grass. He got an old school truck, turned the lights on, and I finished the yard with the headlights showing me the path to cut the grass. Daddy was consistent and I learned not to delay when he asked me to do something again. Daddy's discipline won out over "Batman" that night and I will carry that memory with me much longer than any campy 60's T.V. program. Responsibility was learned in our home under Daddy, even if it was learned the hard way.

(14) Guitar Picking Man

Daddy picked up playing the guitar after the war, by a mail order course and practiced all the time with his brother. Merle Travis, Chet Atkins, and Doc Watson were Daddy's favorite guitarist. Later, he began to like the blues guitar pickers and started going to blues festivals in the Delta. He could pick a tune for anybody and make up lyrics like the "Cockroach Blues" for my daughters when cockroaches scared them, because they had never seen such bugs before. Daddy played at benefits, senior activity centers, and even at church, seeming always to have a song. Some of his favorite songs were "Deep River Blues" by Doc Watson, "China Town" by Chet Atkins, "Roll On Buddy," "Dark as a Dungeon," "I am a Pilgrim," and "Nine Pound Hammer" by Merle Travis. "I am a Pilgrim" was played at his funeral as his coffin was rolled out of church. Daddy always liked everything Johnny Cash sang. "Folsom River Blues" was probably his Cash favorite as well as "Ring of Fire." We grew up singing "That Good Old Mountain Dew." He was a multi-talented Dad and this was just another feature of his life.

My brother Darwin inherited Daddy's guitar skills and continued his legacy of singing with his wife Dana. They have a duet they call "Double Dee." Darwin and Dana have led music at their church and directed the choir in recent years.

(15) Darwin the Guitarist

As mentioned, Darwin is my baby brother who inherited Daddy's musical skills. He and his wife, Dana, have several CDs, do concerts, and sing in cafes. Their musical style is "Country Crossover".

After Daddy died, Darwin gathered some of Daddy's classics on a CD and sent them to me. It was a gift well appreciated that reminded me more and more of Daddy's unique musical ability.

I commend Darwin that after years of coaching, he is making the transition into more of the musical field with his wife, proving again, there is life after coaching.

(16) Daddy was Quite a Fisherman

I never saw my Dad cry except when we were fishing at the McCrae Dead Lake off the Pascagoula River. He hooked a whopper of a Largemouth Bass and was reeling it in, but the 10 lb. test line broke before he could get the fish into the boat. He cried like a baby because he had lost the fish. Throughout the years, he caught many Largemouth Bass, some of which he mounted. However, that was the one he cried tears over when it got away.

Daddy knew where all the good fishing holes were and we fished many of them when I was growing up. He kept up the pace even after he retired and caught all kind of fish, but he especially enjoyed going after Largemouth Bass, which is attested to by the choicest ones being mounted on all our walls.

Daddy loved Agricola and chose to live the rest of his life there because of the abundant hunting and fishing opportunities it provided. He took advantage of these outdoor opportunities to the hilt.

(17) Fluorescent Golf Balls

Daddy attacked golf like he did hunting, fishing, football and played golf all the time at the George County Country Club. My brother Darwin was Golf Coach at George County High School, whose team used the golf course where my Dad played. After school dismissed, he would rush off to the golf course and play through the course.

Daddy purchased some fluorescent golf balls so he could keep playing even after dusk. This persistence illustrated his drive in full force, to keep playing after dark.

Daddy shot a hole in one on Number 3 hole after playing the course hundreds of times and was recognized in the newspaper, as it was verified by those who were playing with him. Most of my vacation time back to Mississippi was spent on that golf course in the latter part of Daddy's life and his passion for golf just proved that he never gave up on outdoor activities.

The last golf round I played with him was quite a test for Daddy. He could hardly stand but he kept going and never stopped. That's the way Daddy was, there was no "quit" in him.

(18) The Carrico's and Coke

The Carrico's were in the United Gas Station with my grandparents in Runnelstown where my parents met. The Carrico's moved to Leakesville later where Daddy coached and taught for five years. We would visit them quite often because of this tie. When we went there, Daddy would tell me, "I bet you'll get a coke." Mrs. Carrico would always pull a Coke or Pepsi out of the refrigerator and serve it with a napkin around it. Sometimes she would pour it on ice then put the napkin around the glass. I never saw anyone serve it that way before or afterwards.

Whenever Daddy would say, "Let's go see the Carrico's," I got in the car eagerly because I knew I would be getting a treat.

(19) My Dad, My Biggest Fan and Cheerleader

Although my Daddy was very busy he was always there for Little League games, and later high school baseball. When I made a good play, he would stand and holler. After hitting three straight bloop singles in an opening game during Little League, he told me at the bench to keep doing that and don't kill the ball. Coming in one day in Babe Ruth league, when I was throwing in from the outfield, he said, "Keep firing the ball in like that." He realized baseball suited me better than football and really encouraged me, always being there and he was never too busy to cheer me on when he could have used that as an excuse not to go to any of my games.

(20) Lorie Burton terrified by the Panther Stories

Lorie Burton was our youngest first cousin of Daddy's sister Carolyn's sons. My aunt named him after my Dad and he visited with our family after I had gone to college and was serving as pastor. I had moved out of the house when this story took place. Lorie came to visit once and stayed with our family for about a week or more. I think he was still living in Natchez and was a little pesky for his age.

I never saw a panther in Agricola and we went to a lot of out-of-the-way fishing places, but Donald tells how he and Daddy got Lorie Burton going spinning tales about panthers in the woods all around them. To hear them tell the stories, it was like living in darkest Africa in the bush. They told him the panthers were fierce and they came out after the rain. It had rained a lot that week when he was with them and that seemed to put Lorie, who was about 12 or 13 at the time on edge.

Donald took a cassette recorder and recorded the closest thing he could get to panther screams, (however he did that). Lorie was sleeping in another bedroom and the windows were open when

Daddy told Lorie they would have to be careful and have the gun loaded to kill those panthers or they would kill every one of us. This exaggeration about the presumed panthers put Lorie on pins and needles.

Donald waited for Lorie to settle down when he went to bed that night. I don't know if Lorie actually went to sleep or not. Donald placed the cassette recorder by the window on full volume causing Lorie to hear what he thought was an attack of a panther. He burst out of the bedroom into my parent's bedroom crying at the top of his lungs, "Uncle Lorie! Get the gun! The panthers are here! Kill them before they kill us!" Between Donald and Daddy, they could have you believing almost anything.

(21) Lemuel caught me

I have always had a vivid imagination and when we were living in a rental house when Agricola High School football was in its glory days, I would go out and pretend to play football, self-broadcasting the games. I have already shared how we used to pretend certain games by real time lineups.

This particular Saturday morning I was just going to town in our yard, pretending a make-believe college team was playing. I was calling the moves, describing the plays, and had my head down when all of a sudden Lemuel Hembree slipped upon the scene unbeknownst to me. His family lived down the road and he was a 9th grader who had been either walking by or riding a bike without me noticing. He cried out, "What are you doing that for?" I was speechless for a moment and very embarrassed. I said the only thing I could say, "I was just pretending."

(22) Preaching is like Coaching

When I shared my call to preach with the church, my Dad did not try to talk me out of it. Instead, he tried to get me to see what I was getting into. He said, "Preaching is a lot like coaching. You will never be able to make everyone happy all the time, because you will please some and make others unhappy. Be true to what you believe and you'll be alright." After over 40 years of dealing with theological problems, which have not been as big as relational problems in the church, I can say with certainty Daddy was right. It has not always been a lovefest, but it has been fulfilling to carry out one's own calling and convictions.

(23) Sometimes I Act Just Like Him

I never tried to be like Daddy, but he has influenced me enough in little habits and ways of expressing myself that have mirrored him. Sometimes my general manner reminds me that I've become just like my Dad and I can't think of a greater compliment.

TOP: Daddy and bird dog, Lucille

LEFT: Largemouth Bass

BOTTOM LEFT: Mama and Daddy in the school office

BOTTOM RIGHT: The Astrodome Trip

TOP LEFT: Daddy as East Central Head Coach

TOP RIGHT: 50th Wedding Anniversary

BOTTOM: Brothers at Anniversary

TOP: Daddy playing the guitar

BOTTOM: Last tribute in church

5.

Courageous Character and Values Taught

The greatest decision my Daddy ever made was to accept Jesus Christ as His Lord and Saviour after he had moved to Agricola. Both he and my mother were baptized in the Agricola Baptist Church. In doing so, they were preparing the way by example for us to trust in Christ as Saviour ourselves.

My mother came from a hard-shell Baptist background and believed in what was called Hyper-Calvinism. My Daddy had a background in a church that went back several family generations. His church taught that you had to be baptized in their church to be a Christian and if you were not baptized at their specific church, you were not a Christian according to them. My Great-Granddaddy on my father's side had donated the land for the church that was built there in Haynesville, Louisiana. You can see how his roots in the church were deep and almost unmovable.

When we moved to Agricola, Daddy's parents got on to him about attending their church and having his family there. We went several times to that church, but really did not feel at home there. My Mother's Daddy, (my Granddaddy) was dying of Leukemia and both he and Daddy were pretty close. It shocked my Daddy to know that Granddaddy told him he was ready to die and be with Jesus. Of course, this ran counter to what Daddy had been taught in the church in which he grew up. My Mother's Dad shared how he had trusted in Christ and according to John 3:16 was ready to go to Heaven because he had placed his faith and trust in Christ for salvation. Daddy knew he did not have that same kind of peace that came from knowing Christ personally and an assurance he would go to heaven when he died. He had not been able to find this peace in his parents' church.

There was a strong pull to stay in the church Daddy was raised in. My other Granddaddy (my father's Dad) had left the Cumberland Presbyterian Church to keep peace in the family through joining my Grandmother's church. However, Daddy knew he wasn't saved and the peace my other Granddaddy had to face death as a believer greatly moved him. The pastor talked with Daddy and he gave his life to Christ as a young adult. Both my Mother and Daddy were baptized in Agricola Baptist, with my brother, David and I old enough to watch and understand their commitment to the Lord. My parent's conversion, baptism and involvement in Agricola Baptist Church set an example that no words can really express.

From then on, our lives were inseparable with church, school, and home and these ingredients became a strong base for family values. Daddy was no hypocrite and he recognized what that was at all times, making earnest efforts not to become one. He befriended Lawrence Baylot, a young preacher who was making quite a stir at Agricola Baptist Church at the time by bringing non-churchgoers to Christ. Brother Baylot loved to hunt and fish so he hung out with Daddy, a lot. I think Brother Baylot really influenced him in a positive way, because several times, I would see Daddy sitting in the car by himself after my Mother had gone home in the other car to cook dinner. He was stunned and shocked by what Brother Baylot preached, particularly related to smoking.

Brother Baylot had a way of expressing himself in the pulpit that was hilarious. He would act out how he met his wife or how a person sucks on a cigarette. The day he did that, I thought the choir was not going to be able to make it through his sermon with a straight face. Brother Baylot influenced the team to pray before games and was the announcer for some home games.

Daddy taught the Junior Boys Sunday School Class at Agricola Baptist Church and after I had accepted Christ a few years later we made our class an evangelistic outpost. We would bring our friends to Christ with Kenny Counselman, (a lifelong friend who is now a medical doctor) and I leading the way. Sunday school was exciting and Daddy would involve the class in a discussion that was always very meaningful. At times, he let Kenny and me sort of lead the class. Daddy was no Bible scholar, but he made everything interesting. He could make the contents of a cake mix interesting if he tried hard enough.

As I progressed through our class, I felt God calling me to preach and Kenny surrendered to a call to missions. Lifelong commitments were made under Daddy when Brother Baylot was our pastor.

We camped out together and had a great time. It was Daddy's influence in the formative years of my life that I shall never forget. When you camp out with your Dad, it means a lot. On one of those trips, we were camping out and then went to sleep in his tent. After everyone was down, a few of the high school boys found out where we were camping and had an electric cattle prong that they used to shock everybody within their tents. What a wakeup call! As mentioned several times already about certain incidents, someone couldn't get away with that today but back then it was just another practical joke.

About this time of church influence, Daddy became the scoutmaster. He was a natural, because he was an outdoorsman. I was a regular at Troop 122 meetings, although I wasn't old enough to be a Boy Scout when we started the troop. Daddy taught the scout laws and made everyone understand the scout oath. He even had prayer with a short devotional at the scout meeting and of course we had fun with all sorts of games in the gym and campouts.

I remember the camporee's and taking home winning ribbons. We went to Camp Tiak in South Forrest County for a couple of weeks in successive years and I was initiated to the Order of the Arrow with others; the special camping organization described earlier. Many of these early Boy Scouts became stars on the football team in Agricola and later at George County High. I'm all in on the Boy Scouts and their influence; I think Boy Scouts were even more meaningful in a country place with nothing much to do besides work on the farms. We learned to appreciate where we lived and Boy Scouts provided a wonderful outlet to enjoy our community, even more so with camping and outdoor activities.

I didn't have enough money for a Boy Scout uniform, but to my Dad where there's a will, there's a way. We got watermelon culls from a local farmer and sold them on the steps of the old Agricola school building that led into the auditorium, when we lived on the campus at what we called the "rat house." We were able to sell enough to get the uniform. One of the greatest values my brothers and I picked up from my parents was that money wasn't as important as family, friends and doing what was right.

We lived in rentals until we finally had a house built on an acre of land that was purchased from Lester Dean for $300. It was up the road from the Browns and Bullards; teachers and principals (in Mr. Bullards' case). We called our little area "Teachersville" because of the unplanned predominance of teachers' homes in such a sparsely populated community. My parents had a house built by Key Realty, in Mobile, Alabama for the hefty sum of $8,500. There was one bathroom for the four of us boys in which we learned to share. This type of arrangement would not have worked if there had been sisters. The little house survived broken windows and scuffles, but we enjoyed living there especially with the one acre we turned into a ball field. We even made our small house into a sports venue which was our version of the Astrodome football games, when both parents went to PTA meetings on Monday nights. We moved the couches back and played touch football. We did this in the time period before the Superdome in New Orleans was built.

Before we moved to Daddy's one and only home, we lived in rentals. We had to leave a rental in the middle of the year and live in the "rat house" which was on the campus of the Agricola school. My bunk bed with David was in the living room and there was one bedroom, a kitchen, and a bathroom (which looked like an afterthought). The train came through each night about 10:00 p.m. and it passed close to the house. It sounded like it was coming through the house every time it passed by. We were so happy to move into our own house, in which our parents lived for 44 years. The house was completely empty when I stayed on for a week after my Mother's funeral service. I thought of how if this house could talk, what kind of memories it would tell. Out of all these experiences, family values were imprinted on our soul through the church, school, and in our home.

We never knew we were poor but the reality of it hit me when I found an old teacher's contract for my mother which was about $6,800 for the entire year of teaching fourth grade in the early 60's.

My brother, Donald, said our parents always made us feel special and if we were poor, we didn't know it. We were rich in so many other things: friends, family, sports and church. I did not know we weren't blessed with much materially because we didn't think about it much as we grew up in Agricola. Donald said, "Our parents used to always do without so we could have something at Christmas and on our birthdays." If we didn't have enough money, they helped us earn money to get something we needed or something that was very special that was worth getting. I remember picking up pecans all day after President Kennedy was killed. That day we did not go to school and I spent the day working in one of the local pecan orchards because I needed to earn enough for Christmas presents.

One long blue station wagon I always loved to see roll up was that of Jack Purvis, Daddy's sporting goods buddy from Jones County, who always did business with Daddy for equipment, uniforms, etc. When he came, Daddy would always manage to get a ball glove, football, or something for us from Jack out of his surplus. He would usually give it to Daddy for his business or drastically cut the price down. Sometimes, we would go to sleep then wake up with a brand new baseball glove right beside us, making it feel like Christmas morning. I'm sure glad I learned from Daddy and my Mother that money can't buy happiness and that it was secondary to the character values they taught so well.

The surprise generosity of my parents continued after I left home for college. I never took any money from them for college. I always had several jobs in the library or cafeteria, (washing dishes). When I was called to Seminary Baptist Church I did not have enough money to buy suits. I went to the local men's clothing store and wanted two suits but just couldn't afford them. I got some at second hand stores but one night in Polk Hall at William Carey College a package came for me. It was a brand new "Matlock special" seersucker suit from my parents. Surprise gifts like that were appreciated much more than money. Their giving spirit to their sons never stopped as I'm sure my brothers could attest to in incidents such as this in their lives.

Most of Daddy's players in sports were of stern stuff and were tough and battle-tested through the hard practices Daddy had with his players. One realization about his players though, was that most of the boys who came out of Agricola and East Central were for the most part honest, forthright, and could be counted on to do the job. Their integrity was usually never in question and I would like to think that much of that came from Daddy's influence and all the things that influenced him.

Adrian Rogers used to say, "You can brag about how good a preacher I am, a good friend, etc., but if you said you don't believe a word I say, you have just cut the taproot out of my character."[5]

---

5 Adrian Rogers, late pastor of Bellevue Baptist Church Memphis TN in a sermon broadcast on the telecast of the churches services on "Love worth Finding."

Daddy's word was as good as his bond and you could always count on Daddy to shoot straight with his players and with people. His character kept him going and kept him strong.

I woke up one morning during our second year in Agricola to hear a man literally cursing Daddy about not playing his son full time and benching him. Daddy remained calm while he stood his ground for not playing the man's son. He never capitulated despite the strong threats from this man. I think the boy did end up making it back to the starting line-up before everything was over, but Daddy never treated this man as an enemy. Instead, he tried to understand him and maintain a friendship with the man. They became good friends after the man accepted Christ and was baptized into the church.

Seeing these events unfold before me over the years, made me see where character really shines through. It cannot be bought and can only be maintained through lifelong commitment, which my Daddy displayed in his life.

6.

EASING OUT BUT NOT EASING UP

How do you back out of coaching? It's an intense job and a lot of coaches have a hard time making the adjustment. For Daddy, it was pretty easy because he had so much going on he didn't have any time to regret not being a head football coach. His career was short compared to many coaches; it was barely 20 years.

I am thankful my brothers and I were deeply influenced by my parents while we were growing up during those formative years. Daddy was a hunter, fisherman, golfer, guitarist, so he just took on another project while letting head coaching and teaching go. He viewed retirement as having more time to hunt, fish, and golf. He loved to take people hunting, and in particular, those who had never done it before. They didn't realize the fast walking that was involved and the amount of skill it takes to shoot birds until they went with Daddy for the first time.

I was never a great hunter and actually my brothers, David and Donald are the ones with that distinction. My Dad was worried when I liked staying home to read and study. He was sure I would grow up to be a "sissy." He told my mother that he needed to take me hunting. To this she replied, "Leave the boy alone, and let him do what he wants." Once, I went squirrel hunting with him. I had the safety off and he discovered it. He said, "Boy, you could have killed us both!" From then on, he was not disappointed when I wanted to stay home and read books.

Daddy always pushed people toward the good in their lives. He was great at encouraging others, which is why his transition to counseling was a natural one. He would try to help students achieve their maximum potential, which was something for which he was very capable.

More trips to the golf course made it a natural thing to do every day. Hunting and fishing intensified and this time his activities were enjoyed with grandchildren and friends. It was like he had come full circle by starting out as an avid sportsman and taking up football coaching. When he let it go, he continued being an avid sportsman, and Daddy was still the same old jovial self he had always been. He carpooled to East Central with Randy Brown, (a neighbor and lifelong friend) and others. They always had a great time commuting, cutting up and sharing together.

Daddy immediately went to work helping Richard Powell at his furniture store in Lucedale after retiring from school altogether. His hiring by the store was shared through a big add in the local paper resulting in many coming by to see him there.

My Dad also picked up a hobby of making ducks out of wood, carving and painting them uniquely to set outside your house by the mail box usually at the end of the driveway. He would put wings on them that would go around and around in a flurry when the wind hit the ducks. He also made quail and other types of birds and became very creative with his wooden birds. You could drive all over Agricola and the surrounding area seeing the ducks and birds he had craved. We even brought one out to California when we returned after our vacation in Mississippi. He used to sell them and say he was putting the proceeds into his retirement fund. I think he really used them for all kinds of golf accessories.

His primary retirement job was as a People Greeter for Wal-Mart. Wal-Mart had just come into Lucedale and was hiring local people, so Daddy was a natural at the job. Outgoing and knowing most everybody in George County, he was introduced to the children and grandchildren of his former students. It became a little difficult to check packages and visit at the same time, but he managed.

It didn't take long for him to get people going and he joked with everybody who came in. A trip to Wal-Mart meant a trip to see Coach Nelson.

The grandkids began to accumulate and he watched them grow up. Donald and Darwin went into coaching high school football. When Donald was head coach at Gautier High School, my younger brother Darwin was a coach at George County High School. My parents walked the tightrope between two teams. When Gautier would play George County, Daddy and my mother would sit on one side for half the game and the other side the next.

One of my visits from California featured a game between both brothers' teams. We sat in lawn chairs behind the end zone with all the former coaches, while my brother Darwin, arranged for all the players to come and congratulate Daddy for being such an example for future generations. I could scarcely hold back the emotions as I pictured everyone Daddy had ever coached standing in line to shake his hand. What a moment in time it was that transcended all generations.

Daddy followed his sons' team as a fan with the same intensity he had coached. When describing my brother Donald's team, he would say, "We did this..." and "We did that..." like he was coaching again.

I really think Daddy enjoyed retirement. Whatever he did, he always approached it full-board with great energy. He did that with his fishing, hunting, and golfing until he was no longer able to do it.

I was with Daddy and my brothers the last week of his life. He subconsciously cast a line out as if he was using a rod and reeling it in again and he would spiral a football, throwing it to some imaginary figure.

He had told my brother that he was going to huddle everybody up a few years before he died when he was obviously hallucinating. Daddy left this life with the energy he had coming into this world and had lived his life.

Both my mother and father had experienced poor health after the turn of the century. My mother had two strokes which left her bedridden until her passing on Easter Sunday in 2007.

Daddy died a year earlier on a Sunday afternoon, January 15, 2006, with the Colts and Steelers playoff game going into overtime. Dying in the overtime of a game was typical for Daddy because he always had a flair for the dramatic and went out that way.

Daddy definitely did not sit back and quit after he retired. He enjoyed every avenue of his life and made life exciting for each of us.

7.

A Powerful Influence

You surely must have noticed the influence Daddy had on all of us. I have shared how my brothers and I do things similar to him with our reactions mirroring his, because those mannerisms and habits are indelibly etched in our minds.

One of the greatest tributes to Daddy was the model he set as a father, coach and as a teacher. All of these roles featured him as a person with courage and determination. That portrait is how we think of our Dad and set the mark in responsibility to a family, making a good situation out of a bad one, and being a person that loves to be around other people.

Daddy's commitment in marriage was real, being married 58 years to my mother, along with other commitments to teaching and coaching for 35 years. He could take anything or anyone and get the maximum potential out of them. When my Dad left us, no one could replace the great void he left behind. We can only try to maintain that same drive in our lives as well.

I've learned to never say we have lost someone at death or that they are gone, because Daddy knew the Lord and accepted Christ. I look forward to seeing him again soon and his influence in our lives really lives on in our families. That influence will always be a part of us in all that we do.

Two truths were startling to me at Daddy's funeral and especially with Mother's passing. When they handed the flag to me being the oldest in my generation, it really hit home. The torch has been passed to the next generation and I am the next in line. This past generation with Daddy's parents, brothers and sisters are gone. I also realize that although they are gone with Daddy, his drive and energy cannot be extinguished in our lives. The game is still on and we are still a part of it, as his sons continue to play it with a full court press.

I found myself going to Daddy's grave the next day after his funeral and saying, "Daddy, I will not let you down or forget you. I will continue doing all God wants me to do because I had a Daddy like you: You were the real deal."

Appendix 1

1968 Championship Remembered

East Central High School has produced many outstanding football teams over the past thirty-seven years. Ten teams in all, have competed in post season play. However, of all the teams to compete on the gridiron, one stands out: The East Central Hornets team in 1968.

The '68 Hornets were molded into a tough, hard-nosed football team by legendary coach L.R. Nelson. Nelson, who came to East Central in 1966 after producing many outstanding teams at Agricola High School, will be forever remembered in the hearts of East Central fans for this 1968 season. During 1968, Coach Nelson's squad would unleash

1968 Records: 10-1 Head Coach: L.R. Nelson		
D'Iberville	13	0
St. Stanislaus	26	40
Leakesville	42	20
St. John	60	0
St. Martin	31	6
Vancleave	60	6
Alba, AL	33	13
Pass Christian	53	13
Baker, AL	33	0
OLV	52	0
Pickle Bowl		
Notre Dame	34	31

an offensive explosion which has not been equaled to this day. This team would finish the season with a 10-1 record and defeat Biloxi's Notre Dame High School in the 1968 Pickle Bowl.

East Central began the season with a 13-0 win over the D'Iberville Warriors. The game was highlighted with two touchdown runs by QB Allen Goff and two interceptions by Mike Long.

Game two would see the Hornets lose their only game of the season by a score of 26-40 at home to St. Stanislaus. With the Hornets leading 26-20 going into the fourth quarter, St. Stanislaus returned a punt 85 yards for a touchdown. Later in the quarter, St. Stanislaus returned two blocked punts for touchdowns to provide the winning margin. East Central would not lose another game that year.

The Hornets would travel to Leakesville next and defeat the Bears 42-20. Goff would throw two TD passes to Mike Long and one to Ronald Kirkwood while scoring one on a four-yard run.

During the next three games the Hornet offense would demonstrate why they are remembered as a devastating machine by outscoring their opponents 151-12. Victories over St. John, St. Martin and Vancleave would exhibit a rushing and passing exhibition. Of particular interest was a 60-6 win over arch-rival Vancleave. Fullback Terrance Wells dazzled the crowd on the night with four touchdown runs. Goff would continue with his assault on the record books while Mike Long continued his scoring barrage.

Wins over Alba (AL), Pass Christian and Baker (AL) would all be by large margins with Goff once again throwing TD passes to his receiving corps of Long, Kirkwood and Rodney Walker.

The final contest of the regular season was billed as a Pascagoula River Conference championship game between OLV and East Central. The Hornets would demonstrate little respect for the highly-touted Eagles as they rolled to a 52-0 win. For the second straight year, L.R. Nelson's Hornets had won the Pascagoula River Conference, but this championship season was not complete. East Central would receive its first ever bowl invitation to meet Notre Dame HS of Biloxi in the 1968 Pickle Bowl at A.L. May Stadium in [Perkinston].

The '68 Pickle Bowl would match the talented Notre Dame Rebels led by future Ole Miss QB Kenny Lyons against the

Hornets. Lyons would be no match for the passing of Goff, the running of Wells and the fleet footed Long as East Central won 34-31. Ronald Kirkwood would catch two TD passes on the night and share game Most Valuable Player honors with QB Allen Goff.

What can be said of the 1968 Hornets? This was a team which set many offensive records which still stand today. Few teams in Mississippi High School history have ever scored 400 points in a regular season. Mike Long set a Mississippi high school record by scoring 142 regular season points and QB Allen Goff became the most gifted passer in East Central history. Although many records were achieved, the best thing that can be said of this team was that it consisted of many fine young men. Is there any wonder why the 1968 East Central Hornets are a team to remember?

Narrative provided by Randy Whitley, a reporter for The Link: A weekly newspaper in Hurley, Mississippi.

Appendix 2
OUT OF THE ASHES

**A Tribute to the undefeated
1963 Agricola Warrior High School Football Team**

Pascagoula River Conference Champions

Coached by L.R. Nelson, my Dad

1963 Coach of Year in the Pascagoula River Conference

Out of the ashes a school and town arose
Determined not to be caught in catastrophic throes

Before the president was shot
A golden era existed in this tiny little spot

It all started with a team unnoticed by all
Coached by my Dad and noted for dominating football

Their season started bleakly in a scoreless tie that day
In a muddy game no one could hardly stand up and play

Then like the school and community after the fire
The team rose to the occasion with determination and grit out of the mire

Eight games played and won, not a one even close
A defense for the ages and an offense turned loose

Players came out of the woodwork so strong and memorable
It seemed they could hardly resemble

A team representing a small school and a small place
But going down in history with such a winning pace

On the field, they steamrolled every opponent
Unphased by not much praise and wonderment

My Dad was coaching his dream team
Barking out the orders and made it hardly seem

There wasn't any struggle to winning and losing was far from their minds
They kept winning and winning leaving the opponents far behind

When the season was over and dust had cleared,
We were given a season and a team we revered

Once in a lifetime a team plays like this
Once in a lifetime our sporting lives are filled with such bliss

That golden season ended a golden era for all who got up off the mat
Life got a lot tougher after that

Things came apart and people were shot
Fires burned, on campuses, riots broke out and tempers got hot

People went to war never to return
Much like a bad dream you wish you could spurn

But that golden season will never be forgot
When my Daddy coached a team that no team could stop

Where are they now? Some may not be even alive
Daddy has gone to his eternal home, no more to joke and jive

And we only remember them and strive to learn what it was like when
        ashes filled our days
Ground to a halt in in our uncertainty about the future with everything
        a haze

Then they came along with Daddy leading the way
Our hopes were restored and night turned to day

There will never be another team like them
And there will never be another coach like my Dad who had no quit in him

That Golden era lives on in our lives for they did so much with so little
of the things they never had
For that was a miracle season that made us joyous instead of sad

Oh, to stay in that era which now is only in our mind
But never let us forget their feats and leave the past behind

They proved anyone could do it no matter how low you sink
You can pick up your life, fallen rescued from the brink

You can be the greatest winner ever when it seems your about to lose
You can overcome anything if you only choose

To play the way they did with passion and with fire
To tell about how we came back and won despite that which would
make you retire

Miracles are possible we lived thru one in that golden year
May we all believe in them because we saw everything turn around
and quench all our fear

The greatest season ever with the greatest team ever did it all
With an example to follow like them we will never lose or fall

The 1963 Agricola Warriors High School Football Team with L.R.
Nelson as their coach

Written by Coach Nelson's oldest son Dan

Appendix 3
Agricola: Where I was raised

Whenever I'm discouraged
and feeling sort of blue
My heart goes back to Agricola
and the times I had with you

I remember the hot summers
and fishing in the ponds all day
I remember the working times
and the field as white as clay

I remember my Grandfather's garden
picking okra early in the morn
and today I sit and wonder
at those days, so peaceful and warm

I remember the baseball field
that we built for my brothers and me
and I remember those games
that I used to play around the tree

I remember the people so compassionate
and warm.
I remember working hard
on a farm.

I remember picking pecans
in an orchard all day
The excitement as we spied a deer
only to have it slip away

I remember long conversations
with my Grandmother at night
The wisdom of her countenance
And her eyes gleaming bright

I remember Mr. Dozier's (My Grandpa)
concern for the lost
As he knelt to pray in the church
he cried for them with great cost

I remember going home to play
with a friend after church.
Going through the country
on a never-ending search.

I remember my shyness
from girls that is
None of them in my house
I'm sure to them I'm a quiz

I remember the countryside
through which I would stroll
The beauty of a sunset
the land would unfold.

I remember loving neighbors
who were close friends
It almost seemed
they were in some way kin.

I remember the fall when
school opened and football began
I remember those teams my father coached
and his determination to win

I remember the spring and
the baseball season I waited so patiently for
I remember preparing all
winter for the season and the car.

I remember our church
Just down the dale.
Where realities were
preached such as heaven and hell

I remember my school
too big for me
I remember coming home,
some peace and quiet to see

I remember the loneliness
of hitchhiking to Lucedale and back
I remember the joy when
a friend picked me up in a hack

I remember my family so
busy yet having time to care
Never letting me think
I wasn't wanted there

I remember our house
not that fancy or nice
Just a home to live in
and place that made you live twice

I remember those starlit
nights when I use to talk to God and dream
about faraway places
and things I had not seen

I remember leaving Agricola
no longer to return
only a memory now
Sometimes something I would spurn

Yet Agricola I cannot leave you,
for in my memory you are always there
Reminding me of times I have spent,
in a place for which I deeply care

Dan Nelson

Appendix 4

No More Whistling at the Bullard's House

There's a ghostly silence at the Bullard's house
Although I'm not there to hear
I can imagine though as I
grew up with my family so near.

My mother called to share Mr. Bullard
is now with the Lord.
No more whistling over at the Bullard's house
no more whistling in his yard.

But Oh, the heritage that is left behind
of a hard-working versatile man.
A man who was a true neighbor
A man who was a true friend

Whether it was whistling while he worked
and he did plenty of that all day
or whether it was hunting, fishing, or teaching
you knew he enjoyed life in every way

To see that zest, that goodness
that came from him all the time
Is rare in this day and age
For many to hope to find.

Once he spoke in my small country church where I was pastor.
about the Lord and he talked of him aglow
But most of all I remember his faithfulness
The love of Christ he did show

He was a rock in his home church
A pillar of strength till the end
A wise sage to talk with.
A wonderful man a true friend.

He appreciated my father
and helped my mother in every way
He coached my brothers in all sports
and encouraged me for this I cannot repay.

And I still imagine I'm back in Agricola
waking up on a bright sunny morn
Hearing that whistling Mr. Bullard
A hoeing in the corn.

That man as strong as steel
will be missed by the small and great
By his wonderful daughters and wonderful wife,
committed now to his eternal fate

And it won't be the same
without whistling Mr. Bullard's form
Working in his garden
No worry it seemed, no alarm.

Oh, but in heaven we'll see him
and all who've gone before
And we'll hear that sweet whistling
as we enter in for ever more

Dan Nelson

Appendix 5

Closing Reading at my Father's Funeral
January 17, 2006

What more can we say
What more can we do
All that I am
is all because of you
Your task has been completed
Your life has been spent
It is time to say a final good-bye
and say a thank you for all you have meant
We are grateful for the things we have learned
They will be with us to our dying day
They will a part of future generations
That will live to say
What a father you have been
What a master coach that we and others have had
What a dedicated husband you've been to a faithful wife
What a teacher, what a friend, What a wonderful life
We are your legacy
We are what you have wrought
Every time we turn around we will remember what you've taught
We shall never forget you
We will carry what we learned from you deep inside
It will be more than enough to sustain us
Till we once again meet on the other side

Dan Nelson

PICTURE CAPTIONS

Pictures found on pages 29-31:

- Daddy's World War II picture that was turned into a painting.

- My Mother and Father as newlyweds.

- A 50's picture in Leakesville and the deer Daddy shot that day. It was his most productive day ever deer hunting.

- One of Daddy's successful girls' basketball teams at Leakesville High School.

- A picture of Father and Mother with Uncle Carol and Aunt Willie Nelson.

- An early picture of our family before Darwin was born, when we first moved to Agricola.

- The first team Daddy had at Agricola. They finished 6-4 that year which was not bad for a school who had just started a football program two years prior. The old helmets reveal their early equipment.

- The various assortments of equipment we had with the Pee Wees. The other guys in the back of them didn't have equipment, while some of the linemen were barefooted. They were able to get castoffs from the High School team but it didn't diminish their scrap.

- What a motley crew! Another Agricola Pee Wee Football team picture with some very memorable characters in the shot before they went on to high school football.

- What a hole to go through for a touchdown against Harrison Central. This picture shows Jimmy (Foots) Davis scoring a touchdown during the 1962 football season. You could drive a truck through it. The team was 7-3 that year but lost the Turkey Bowl in Ocean Springs.

Pictures found on pages 63-66:

- This is the famous undefeated team of 1963 that made it all happen. These were great players in a dream season. They gave up only 13 points all season long and won the Pascagoula River Conference that year undisputed. Daddy was awarded the *Coach of the Year* for the Conference.

- This is the famous East Central Team of 1968 who won the Pascagoula River Conference and the Pickle Bowl. Several players went on to college from this team. They were explosive in their offense scoring over 400 points that season.

- A force to reckon with: Jimmy Vise, the offensive and defensive tackle in Daddy's early teams at Agricola. He once finished a game with a broken leg. This picture infers, "Watch out you're going get hit real hard by Jimmy."

- Daddy in one of his famous poses as a coach. He loved football and enjoyed coaching the sport.

- Dozier Rogers (our Grandpa) who was a great soul-winner and deacon in the Baptist Church for 54 years. He was a great Man of God and encourager to me in the ministry.

- Coaches, press clippings, and an awarded player: Mike Wade and the schedule of the famous undefeated Agricola Warrior team of 1963.The coaches left to right are: Buddy Howard, Daddy and Charles McMullan.

- This is a much earlier picture of my brothers and I, ranging in age from about 12 to 3.

- Here is the Pee Wee team of the 1963 season when the high school team went undefeated and won the conference championship. I'm in there on first row on the left. I may have been small, but I was fast.

Pictures found on pages 107-109:

- Daddy's hunting prowess with Bobwhite Quail is seen in this picture. He hunted with Lucille, a Springer Spaniel pictured here with Daddy.

- Let's not forget the Largemouth Bass, like these which Daddy caught somewhere in Agricola.

- Our Father and Mother are pictured here together in the School Office. They both taught in the Mississippi school system for decades.

- A picture taken during the family vacation in Houston while going to a game at none other than the Astrodome. Looks like I'm the only one who didn't get an Astro's T-shirt. I'm beginning to kick up my heels as a teenager it seems.

- Daddy as East Central Head Coach probably year of the '68 Championship season.

- The 50th Wedding Anniversary Celebration showing my Dad and Mom cutting their cake in 1997.

- A picture is of the brothers all grown up at the Anniversary Celebration: From right to left: (Me), David, Donald and Darwin.

- Daddy never stopped picking the guitar, even in retirement, pictured here at the County Senior Center.

- One of Daddy's last recognitions as a World War II Veteran was caught in picture at Agricola Baptist Church.

BACK COVER PICTURE

Captured in time is the best moment of Agricola High School Football up to that point. Finishing their 3rd season and the 2nd under Daddy as coach, they are awarded the Camellia Bowl Trophy in Lucedale, Mississippi for beating the Richton Rebels 32-12, finishing with a 9-2 record despite the memorable loss to Rocky Creek.

About the Author

DAN NELSON has served as pastor of First Baptist Church of Camarillo, California, in the greater Los Angeles area for the last 33 years. He has also served as pastor of First Baptist Church Burney, California, and Seminary Baptist Church of Hintonville, Mississippi. Dan has served in the Northwest Baptist Convention for two years as Associate to the Evangelism Director in Portland, Oregon. He has also worked as an evangelist through the California Baptist Convention in Fresno on student-led revival teams. Dan has preached in over 40 evangelistic meetings and revivals in his ministry.

Dan is a native of Mississippi, being born in Hattiesburg having grown up in Agricola. He holds the Doctor of Ministry degree from Southwestern Baptist Theological Seminary in Fort Worth, Texas, a Ph. D. degree from California Graduate School of Theology in Glendale, California, and the Master of Divinity degree from New Orleans Baptist Theological Seminary in New Orleans, Louisiana. He attended Golden Gate Baptist Theological Seminary in Mill Valley, California, for a year and graduated from William Carey University in Hattiesburg, Mississippi with a B.A. degree.

He has been married to his wife Janice for 42 years. They have two daughters Krista and Kimberly living in Texas and Oregon. Dan is an active contributor to blog sites and publications with various articles. He is a regular contributor to "SBC Today" with many articles on biographies, sermons and topical studies. He is an avid bicyclist and an instructor in indoor cycling (spin class) at several local gyms.

Dan has been active in the Southern Baptist Convention denominational structure, serving on the Board of Trustees at Southwestern Baptist Theological Seminary in Fort Worth, Texas, and as National Alumni Chairman for New Orleans Baptist Theological Seminary in New Orleans, Louisiana.

His first book, *Baptist Revival: Reaffirming Baptist Principles in Today's Changing Church Scene* was published in 2016. He is awaiting the publication of his next book: *A Burning Shining Light: The Testimony and Witness of George Whitefield.*

CPSIA information can be obtained
at www.ICGtesting.com
Printed in the USA
FFOW01n1924010317
33000FF